THE MAN WHO WAS M

OTHER BOOKS BY ANTHONY MASTERS

THE MAN WHO WAS M

The Life of
MAXWELL KNIGHT

Anthony Masters

///

Basil Blackwell

© Anthony Masters 1984

First published 1984

Basil Blackwell Publisher Ltd
108 Cowley Road, Oxford OX4 1JF, UK

Basil Blackwell Inc.
432 Park Avenue South, Suite 1505,
New York, NY 10016, USA

British Library Cataloguing in Publication Data

Masters, Anthony
  The man who was M.
  1. Knight, Maxwell   2. Spies——Great Britain——Biography
  I. Title
  327.1'2'0924   UB271.G72K5

  ISBN 0-631-13392-5

Library of Congress Cataloging in Publication Data

Masters, Anthony, 1940–
  The man who was M.

  Bibliography: p. 203
  Includes index.
  1. Knight, Maxwell. 2. Intelligence officers—Great Britain—Biography. 3. Intelligence service—Great Britain—History—20th century. I. Title.
  UB271.G72K556 1984   327.1'2'0924 [B]   84-18403
  ISBN 0-631-13392-5

Typeset by Katerprint Co. Ltd, Oxford
Printed in Great Britain by
The Camelot Press Ltd, Southampton

CONTENTS

To my wife, Robina, for her continuous help and involvement, my agent, Michael Sissons, for his wise counselling, and my editor, John Davey, for his patience and encouragement. Also to the memory of Max himself.

ACKNOWLEDGEMENTS

I WOULD like to thank the following friends and associates of Maxwell Knight who gave me so much willing assistance in writing this biography.

Mrs. John Baber, John Bingham, Madeline Bingham, the late Anthony Blunt, Peggy Blockey, Jeffrey Boswall, Andrew Boyle, Dr. Maurice Burton, Bruce Campbell, John Clegg, John Costello, Tony Dale, Richard Darwall, Margery Fisher, the Rt. Hon. Michael Foot, Malcolm Frost, Jonathan Fryer, Mrs. Goddard Wilson, Pamela Gray, Joan Gray, Olga Gray, Edward Greene, Paul Greene, Richard Griffiths, Jeffrey Hamm, Robert Harris, Leo Harrison Matthews, Desmond Hawkins, Kathleen Hocking, Sir Eric St. Johnston, Mrs. Cecil Kaye, Henry Knight, the Librarians of Christ Church, Oxford, Adrian Liddell-Hart, Joan Littlewood, David Lloyd, David McClintock, Cyril Mills, Margaret Moller, the Hon. Lady Mosley, Max Mosley, Nicholas Mosley, Dr. Ernest Neal, Terence Padmore, Christopher Parsons, Stanley Peck, Joanna Phipps, Alan D. M. Ramsay, Hilda F. Rendle, Tom Roberts, Ian Sayer, Mrs. G. Selsey, Mrs. H. N. Southern, Diana Smith, Harry Smith, Colonel Robin Stable, Dorothy Stanton, David Streeter, Derek Tangye, Lois Taylor, Molly Tucker, Leslie von Goetz, Nigel West, Anthony Wheatley, Pamela Wilson, Philip Wacher, Joan Wooton, Sir John Younger.

In particular I would like to thank Winwood Reade for her perceptive understanding of Maxwell Knight as well as her interest in the manuscript, and John Cooper, a profound admirer of Max's contribution to natural history, who has also helped me to put his elusive personality into perspective.

CHRONOLOGY

1900   Maxwell Knight born in Mitcham, Surrey
1915   Enrolled on HMS *Worcester*
1917   Joins the Royal Naval Reserve
1918   Arrives in America
1919   Ministry of Shipping
1920   School-teaching and socializing
1924   Recruited into M.I.5
1925   Marries Gwladys Poole
1930   The recruitment of Olga Gray
1934   Publishes *Crime Cargo*
1935   Death of Gwladys
1935   Publishes *Gunman's Holiday*
1937   The Office opens in Dolphin Square
1938   Trial of the Woolwich Arsenal spies
1938   Marries Lois Coplestone
1939   The recruitment of Joan Miller
1940   Trial of Tyler Kent and Anna Wolkoff
1940   Mosley interned
1940   Ben Greene interned
1941   Driberg exposed by Blunt and sacked from
       the Communist Party
1944   Annulment of marriage to Lois Coplestone
1944   Marries Susi Barnes
1946   Begins a new career in broadcasting as a
       natural historian
1956   Leaves M.I.5
1968   His death

PROLOGUE

MAXWELL KNIGHT was an enigma: occultist, spy, naturalist, lover at a distance, with many acquaintances but few friends. This has made piecing his life together from the written and verbal accounts of those who knew him both difficult and fascinating. Knight was very much a natural spy, carefully protecting himself by dividing his life into separate compartments and playing several contrasting roles with astonishing virtuosity.

Readers will be able to judge for themselves how far I have been able to penetrate Knight's personality. In any event, the account of what he did and of the people and great events concerned seems to me to have been worth telling. I hope that it will be found so.

ANTHONY MASTERS

Come, seeling night,
Scarf up the tender eye of pitiful day,
And with thy bloody and invisible hand,
Cancel and tear to pieces that great bond
Which keeps me pale! Light thickens, and the crow
Makes wing to the rocky wood;
Good things of day begin to droop and drowse,
Whiles night's black agents to their preys do rouse.

Macbeth, III.ii

As he crawled beside the kerb up through Hyde Park, the slow drumbeat of his two-inch exhaust keeping him company, he felt excited at the prospect of his interview with M, the remarkable man who was then, and still is, head of the Secret Service. He had not looked into those cold, shrewd eyes since the end of the summer.

Reflections by James Bond in Ian Fleming's *Live and Let Die* (Jonathan Cape, 1954)

Fieldcraft does not only mean stalking, camouflaging and the making of hides. It also means knowing where to find what you are looking for, at what seasons and times to look; how to deal with what you have found if you want to catch it.

Maxwell Knight, *The Young Field Naturalist's Guide* (G. Bell, 1952)

CHAPTER ONE

SENT TO SEA: 1900–1918

CHARLES HENRY MAXWELL KNIGHT was born on 4 September 1900 in Mitcham, Surrey. His family was impoverished, thanks to the selfishness of his father. Hugh Knight's spendthrift ways, which included regular visits to the south of France with a series of mistresses, had slowly bankrupted his practice as a solicitor. He expected constant help from his eldest brother, Robert, of Tythegston Court in Glamorgan, an academic who lived frugally but held the strings of the substantial family purse. Robert was devoted to his house and saved every penny for fear of losing it: his obsessive economy was in part a reaction to the prodigal behaviour of his ancestor, the Reverend Robert Knight, who had run up such spectacular debts that Tythegston and its estate nearly had to be sold. This narrow-minded Welsh Knight and his children overshadowed Max's early life.

Ada Knight, Max's mother, was a plump, blowsy, good-humoured woman, given to annoying the effete Robert by asking racy questions and giving great bellows of uncouth laughter. Cecil Kaye, one of Robert's daughters, and a playmate of Max's, remembers her Aunt Ada as 'very fat and vulgar. As children we loved her because she was floppy and said outrageous things to my father like "Who did you kiss last night?" She was full of fun and jokes – all of which continually shocked my parents.'

Ada had a son, Cyril, from a previous marriage, as well as

three children from her marriage to Hugh. Eric was eight years older than Max, and Enid was six years older. The family's financial straits frequently sent them to stay at Tythegston for short periods. From her own family's point of view Cecil Kaye recalled that her sister, her two brothers and herself were deeply happy at home. Nevertheless, looking back, she realized that, although her father was generous to his tenant farmers and their dependents, both her parents shared the prejudices and conventions of their class. They disapproved of Hugh's philandering as much as they disapproved of Ada's vulgarity. As for the children, Eric and Enid were found acceptable because they were conventional but in his early childhood Max was considered 'different' – a child they could not categorize, an individualist. Nevertheless, financial help was available for Eric and Max, provided they toed the line.

Although Robert's two sisters, Katherine and Frances, led orthodox lives, their brother Charles was another black sheep. He was considered an even greater disgrace to the family than Hugh and was rarely mentioned by Robert. Once a brilliant organist at the parish church of Mayfield in Sussex, Charles died both unmarried and alcoholic.

In Robert's time Tythegston Court was falling into disrepair, partly because of his strict economies. In spite of this neglect, the building was elegant, based on an early medieval tower house and a Tudor manor. The Knights, as prosperous Bristol merchants, had inherited Tythegston in 1732 through an advantageous marriage settlement. Towards the end of the eighteenth century a portico was added and a new east front built. The spacious lawns and estates greatly appealed to Max after the genteel poverty of Mitcham, with his father's interminable financial crises, infidelities, and expensive holidays in retreat from the family, matched by his mother's determination to laugh everything off. This was a difficult atmosphere for a child to grow up in, and although Eric and Enid were more resilient, Max was clearly made both deeply miserable and insecure. He responded by turning to the animal world as a refuge from the human environment that had proved so unsatisfactory. Cecil Kaye remembers this vividly:

> He had an all-absorbing interest in caterpillars and he would spend hours observing them. I rather liked him, although he seemed withdrawn and tried almost too hard to please adults. With insects and animals he was quite different, for he was very knowledgeable; he handled them brilliantly and they seemed to come to him easily, trustingly.

Although Cecil was a few years younger, Max accepted her as a companion and they used to explore the sea-shore together. But Cecil never became a bosom friend and she soon discovered that 'he was very close to his sister Enid and he didn't seem to want anyone else to get near.'

As he grew older, Max Knight tended to live in three different worlds: the troubled Mitcham house, his private day school, where an aptitude for games gave him confidence, and Tythegston, where his love of nature could be given full rein, the adults being kept at bay by his ingratiating manners.

His relationship with his parents became increasingly difficult. His father's involvement with his mistresses made him a distant figure, with little influence on his children. Ada Knight hid her real feelings behind a mask of brash joviality and was unable to reach out to her introverted son, who had already developed his own protection against being hurt. In 1914 Max's father died suddenly at the age of only fifty-three. Although this did not affect Max deeply, for his father had always been a remote figure, it did bring about a significant change in his life style.

Robert, already dissatisfied with Max, detecting a certain amount of rebelliousness in his withdrawn attitude, decided to provide him with the basis for a safe and honourable career by sending him to H.M.S. *Worcester*.

Combining the roles of public school and training ship, the *Worcester* had a reputation for taking boys who were 'difficult' and putting them through a highly disciplined, arduous curriculum that was designed to turn them out as responsible citizens. Robert felt the *Worcester* would be extremely good for Max, who in autumn 1914 entered this new world of independence and hardship with considerable caution.

Known as the Incorporated Thames Nautical Training College, the *Worcester* was permanently anchored on the River Thames off Greenhithe in Kent. The old three-deck, three-masted sailing ship, a relic of Napoleonic times, was linked to the shore by a long, narrow jetty. Controlled by the Elder Brethren of Trinity House, and run by Captain David Wilson-Barker, R.N., a man of uncertain temper, the ship was heavily subsidized by shipping companies such as the P. & O., the Union Castle and the Blue Funnel, and its job was to train future officers for the merchant navy. Although conventional school subjects were taught, practical seamanship was an important element and instruction in tying knots, navigation, signalling and sailing became more predominant as the boys progressed through the classes. The clanging of bells marked the hours of the day, the bosun's pipe summoned the pupils to prayers or assemblies, and at least half an hour a day was devoted to nautical tasks such as scrubbing decks, polishing brass or raising and lowering boats.

The open upper deck, between poop and forecastle, was used for exercise; the galley, mess and masters' cabins lay below the poop, while below the forecastle the cadets had their own mess. Between the two was the main deck, a versatile area used as an assembly point, divided by movable partitions into six class-rooms during school hours, and becoming a common-room or indoor games room in the evenings and at weekends. Dormitories, where the cadets slept in hammocks, were on the lower deck, and below that, on the tier deck, were bathrooms and boat repair workshops. The hold was used as a gym or a concert hall, and this completed the romantic but spartan environment –

except for the rigging which rose to dizzy heights, climbed by cadets on ceremonial occasions.

Baths were limited to one a week and the most primitive aspect of life on the *Worcester* was the washing arrangements, which consisted of ice-cold water drawn on unheated decks, with heads (lavatories) so chilly that no cadets lingered in them long. The food was grim; the writer Dennis Wheatley, who was on the *Worcester* two years before Knight and later became one of his closest friends, described the menu in the following terms:

> For breakfast, coarse porridge, bread, margarine, and the cheapest possible marmalade; for midday dinner, meat so bad that at times it actually stank, followed most days by suet puddings in which there were globules of solid fat as large as currants; for tea, bread, maragarine and nonde-script, unpalatable jam; for supper, a mug of watery cocoa with spots of oil floating on top, and iron-hard ship's biscuits.[1]

Knight's first encounter with the *Worcester* was made in the shadow of the beginning of the First World War. He was taken to his interview with Captain Wilson-Barker by his Uncle Robert, and there he learnt that the *Worcester* was considered to be the equivalent of a first-rate public school with nautical additions and that, providing he buckled to, his abilities might take him far. After a visit to the outfitters, Da Silva's, where Knight was measured for mess kit, uniform and the everyday clothing of blue cloth trousers and blue serge sweaters, he began his first term with some trepidation. His parting from Enid was a tremendous wrench, but there were few other regrets. His mother, who had taken his father's death with equanimity, was already comfortably moulding herself into widowhood, coming to depend on Enid, not only as a spinster daughter but also as a breadwinner. Eric, much against Enid and Ada's wishes, had

---

[1] *The Young Man Said: Memoirs, 1897–1914* (Hutchinson, 1977).

volunteered to join the army, which of course pleased Robert, who felt he had 'done the right thing'. Knight, who had never been close to his brother, vaguely agreed. He did not miss Mitcham or Tythegston, except for his explorations of natural history; he went to H.M.S. *Worcester* with apprehensive curiosity and a sense of starting a new life.

At first the routine exhausted him completely, but gradually he began to adapt to it. Taught by teachers for academic subjects and instructors for nautical ones, he soon found that he had an aptitude for both disciplines. He became part of a 'top' or division of fifteen boys, over which a cadet petty officer held prefectorial sway. All cadets on the *Worcester* were divided into two watches – port and starboard – and it was from these watches that the divisions were made up. Knight, who was tall for his age and naturally athletic, became a strong member of the duty crews who rowed the captain, staff and visitors ashore, took part in races with the long whalers belonging to the ship, learnt how to row and cox a boat, how to sail, navigate and climb the rigging. He returned home after his first term splendidly equipped with holiday uniform, his caps adorned with gold badges. The even more glamorous mess kit gave each cadet, however puny, a certain *élan* at local dances, with its gold-braided bumfreezer black jacket, white waistcoat, gold buttons and tight black trousers. Dressed in such style, Knight was the toast of Mitcham, and at Tythegston Uncle Robert was heard to remark that 'at least the boy looks the part.' From him, this was high praise indeed.

With not only Eric but also Robert's sons, Henry and John, fighting in France, there was considerable tension at both Mitcham and Tythegston. Every day Ada and Robert expected to hear the worst; every day their nerves were stretched a little bit further. On the *Worcester*, younger staff departed to the trenches and the mounting death roll of old boys was read out by Captain Wilson-Barker on the main deck each week. Despite all this, Knight was scarcely touched by the tragic scale of events outside the little world of the *Worcester*. The war was tinged

with romantic heroism; it introduced him to the ever-resource-
ful Hannay in *The Thirty-Nine Steps* (1915) and *Greenmantle*
(1916). He fell in love with Buchan's racy, jingoistic writing and,
in his fantasy world, he too raced through the Scottish heather
with Richard Hannay, bent on routing all foreigners and
keeping the Union Jack flying on good English soil. It is ironic
that Buchan was to become M.I.5's press liaison officer in 1917,
after serving as an intelligence officer at the front in France.
When describing his memories of M.I.5 in his autobiography,[2]
Buchan exactly encapsulates the appeal this type of atmosphere
always had for Knight, first of all in the attraction of the Hannay
image and later in his love of the clandestine. 'I have some queer
macabre recollections of those years – of meeting with odd
people in odd places, of fantastic duties which a romancer would
have rejected as beyond probability.'

But if Knight saw the war in a hazy, somewhat romantic light,
he recognized the *Worcester* as a jungle in which, if he was to
survive at all, he must be king. His father had been too remote a
figure to love or to mourn, but his early departure contributed
to Knight's feeling that he was different: he was alone. At home
this isolation could still be assuaged by his devotion to the
animal kingdom, but he was cut off from this on the *Worcester*;
instead, Knight concentrated on developing physical and techni-
cal prowess.

The pecking order gave each cadet three alternatives: to be a
rabbit and be bullied, to plod and be accepted, or to achieve and
dominate. Petty officers were picked because they were good
all-rounders, and this rank Knight had been determined to reach
from his first few weeks on the ship. But the climb was arduous.

The *Worcester*'s fagging system was unique. All new cadets in
their first year were known as 'new shits' and each senior cadet
could command their services at any time, although not on a
personal basis. In the second year the 'new shits' became 'old
hands' and, although they were not entitled to give orders to
fags, they could no longer be fags themselves. As a result,

[2] *Memory Hold the Door* (Hodder and Stoughton, 1940).

7

relieved that they were no longer in the lowest grade, they in their turn bullied the first years unmercifully.

Homosexuality existed on the ship as much as it did in an average public school. The 'new shits' tended to make strong, sometimes physical, friendships in adversity, but these rarely lasted into the middle period of their schooling. Some of the older boys acquired 'jams' – short for the bastard French term *jamoirs* – attractive younger boys whom they would kiss and fondle but rarely take to their beds. It is hardly surprising that senior boys, having associated with girls in the holidays and then spending the term cooped up for three months on a small boat exclusively with their own sex, sometimes sublimated their sexual desires into romantic feelings for younger boys.

The school's initiation test was no worse than in many conventional public schools and, according to its lights, at least meted out rough justice, as well as rewarding physical and psychological courage. The test was described as 'new shits singing' and was conducted in the hold on the evening of the Saturday nearest half-term. Although not a physical coward, Knight looked ahead to this event with trepidation, for it would be the first time he would have to prove himself, and he hoped it would give him a foundation for the rise to success he coveted. If he flunked this, he would be tainted for the rest of his training-ship career.

The ceremony was elaborate. The prefects sat gravely on the stage, the rest of the cadets on wooden tiers, and the sixth-termers (those who had been on the *Worcester* for three years) formed two lines on either side of a number of padded gym mats. Each of these cadets held in his hand a piece of rope, knotted at the bottom.

The ceremony then began, with the 'new shits' forming a worried line at the opposite end of the mats to the prefects. Then, one by one, and to the accompaniment of a hearty chorus of 'What shall we do with the drunken sailor?' each wretched 'new shit' was thrown on to the mat and had to crawl through a barrage of knotted ropes towards the stage. Then he had to stand on a three-legged stool, sing a popular song and finally be tipped back on to the mat to take a second beating as he crawled back to the next luckless victim. In some cases, if the 'new shit' had pulled his weight during the term or had shown courage while crawling or singing, he would not be tipped back on to the mat but would be allowed to return in glory to his group. This Knight was determined to achieve, and despite the pain of quite a vicious beating he reached the stage and sang 'It's a long way to Tipperary'. He was allowed to stagger back to his fellows with the sixth-termers cheering him for his courage, his singing and the involvement he had already shown. Knight had arrived.

By the time he was sixteen, Knight had reached nearly six feet in height. He was thin, dark-haired, with a narrow face, projecting ears and slightly feminine, delicate features. His ambitions at the *Worcester* had been fulfilled: he had shone at school work, at nautical studies, at boating and at sport. He had used all his varied natural talents and had earned the praise of teachers, instructors and cadets alike. In addition, he was well on his way to becoming a petty officer.

In the holidays, however, he reverted to his absorption with natural history and few of his qualities of leadership were apparent. As a result, Robert, who received copies of his reports, was amazed to see his nephew described in such glowing terms, and was at a loss to associate the introverted, nature-loving boy he knew at Tythegston with the very model of an up-and-coming young naval officer he read about from H.M.S. *Worcester*. Enid was the only one who really understood her brother. He would confide in her and she was still his sounding-board. Eventually, however, Knight's double life began to disturb her and she too found it hard to associate the gentle introvert with the successful all-rounder. She began to realize, with mounting unease, that Knight had learnt how to separate his life into compartments and to act out roles for himself that both satisfied him and utterly convinced those around him. She also detected a driving ruthlessness in his role-playing. His way of compensating for his own inadequacies and feelings of isolation was simply going all out to win. Enid tried to advise him, but he brushed her admonitions gently aside, implying that a Mitcham seamstress was quite unable to advise a potential petty officer.

In 1916, just as Knight had reached this rank, it was announced that his brother Eric had been killed in action. Ada and Enid were shattered but Knight had not been close to Eric and, according to Cecil, appears to have felt no great sense of personal loss. He did, however, see him as having died a hero's death and, much to Enid's and his mother's dismay and Robert's amazement, felt prompted to volunteer for war service.

Although he was only seventeen and still in the third year of his studies on the *Worcester*, Knight was not unique in volunteering. Many boys of his age had already done so, and Captain Wilson-Barker did not discourage them, for mixed reasons of patriotism and public relations on behalf of his training ship.[3] In September 1917, Knight left the *Worcester* and spent the last year of the war as a midshipman in the Royal Naval Reserve, in armed trawlers and later armed merchantmen. The trawlers had been armed with guns and equipped with mine-seeking gear. Asdic sound equipment had also been fitted for anti-submarine patrols. Fish-holds became mess-decks and these tiny, under-equipped boats were plunged into war.

John Bingham, one of Knight's senior colleagues in M.I.5 during the Second World War, while admiring his leadership, has said that 'although he was not a physical coward, I never thought of him as front-line officer material.' Knight's year of war was cold, wet and arduous but not designed to test the truth of Bingham's statement, for he saw little of the enemy. Life on the trawlers was certainly unpleasant, and it was not much better when he was transferred to a merchantman, but Knight never had to face the bloody carnage of the battlefields and the filth and disease of the trenches which fell to the lot of so many young men of his age. Despite the primitive conditions at sea, he was still able to maintain intact his vaguely romantic notions of war.

[3] The *Worcester* was taken out of commission at the beginning of the Second World War. The *Exmouth* (renamed the *Worcester*) replaced it in 1945, but was sold in 1978 to be broken up.

Most of the young officers in the Royal Naval Reserve were put in command of crews of fishermen, tugboat men and lightermen. Records at the National Maritime Museum indicate that many of these crews wanted the war to end, partly because they were impatient with their new young officers, and partly because they simply wanted to go home. But the young men of the R.N.R., of whom Knight was typical, had dreams of heroic sea-battles – perhaps a second Trafalgar in which they would gallantly vanquish the foe. In fact, the British and German fleets met only once – at the Battle of Jutland. Much of the remainder of the First World War's naval action involved blockade and counter-blockade. Nevertheless, British sea-power played an important part in the defeat of Germany and, without it, the minute British Expeditionary Force of 1914 would not have been able to expand into a substantial army by 1918.

When Knight joined the R.N.R. in 1917, 869,000 tons of British, Allied and neutral shipping had been sunk (largely by German U-boats) in April of that year alone. This brought the total lost since the beginning of 1917 to 2,360,000 tons – a massive proportion of the 4,000,000 tons sunk since the opening of hostilities. The trawler and merchantmen patrols were therefore vital, for the Germans had determined to shatter Britain's navy by the use of U-boats. Britain had responded with mine-laying, as well as the skilful use of her own submarines, airships and planes. Merchant ships were given much heavier defensive armaments and specific routes were laid down for their passage, so that protection could be given by smaller armed ships.

Towards the end of hostilities in 1918, while serving on an armed merchantman, Knight spent a few days in New York. It was an experience that he never forgot. The openness of American people was a sharp contrast to the reserve and inhibition of the English (in particular the Knights of Tythegston), and he felt more free than he had ever felt before. His brief leave was further enlivened by the patronage of a rich American, who met the young sailors in a bar and offered to show them the sights. He also paid their expenses. Knight and his compatriots had a tremendous time, during which their patron introduced them to jazz – an event that was to have a profound effect on Knight's musical tastes. So enthralled was he by this new musical experience that he later learnt to play the drums, the clarinet and the saxophone. Jazz as a pastime became one of his obsessions, second only to his passion for natural history. Most of his domestic animals (including snakes, bush-babies and parrots) were brought up on a musical diet of Sidney Bechet. Indeed, Knight claimed to have met Bechet, although when reminiscing to Margery Fisher, the distinguished children's book critic and wife of the eminent writer and naturalist the late James Fisher, there was possibly a little exaggeration when he told her that while in America he 'had once had lessons on the saxophone with Sidney Bechet'. He also told her of 'how he sat next to a quiet man at a concert, fell into conversation with him during the interval and discovered he was one of the Marx brothers.'

Knight regretfully returned to his ship at the end of the leave and gloomily contemplated his future. The war was coming to an end and, despite his training on the *Worcester*, he saw no reason to pursue a career in the merchant navy. But the alternatives seemed nebulous and the thought of his uncle's disapproval depressed him further. Knight had absolutely no idea of how or where to apply his many talents.

When the war ended he was discharged from the R.N.R. with little personal experience of the harsh realities of the war and its long-term effects. If he had fought on the bloody loam of France, shivering in water-filled, rat-infested ditches, watching men dying all around him, perhaps he would have been disillusioned, as so many were, and felt that England was an unfit land for heroes to return to. Participation on the fringe, however, had not lessened his enthusiasm for adventure, and his spirit of nationalism, reinforced by his early training on the *Worcester*, was undiminished.

CHAPTER TWO

MOVING INTO SOCIETY: 1918–1930

To Robert Knight's fury, his nephew left the merchant navy at the end of the First World War, and served a miserable year as a clerk in the Ministry of Shipping. The work was dull and uninspiring and, in 1920 Max left, telling his uncle that his reason for doing so was that he had endured four years of naval discipline – three on the *Worcester* and one with the R.N.R. – and uninspiring and in 1920 Max left, telling his uncle that his America had made him realize how little he had seen of life, so he came out of the Ministry into a world that he knew nothing about and for which he had little training. Robert reacted by withdrawing his support, exclaiming that he had wasted his money on his nephew's education; he declared him another black sheep. Max was no longer welcome at Tythegston and would certainly have to look elsewhere for money or other help.

Unabashed, Knight started hunting for a job and eventually found one, teaching Latin and games at a prep school in Putney in south-east London. Unable to keep up the house at Mitcham any longer, Ada and Enid moved with him to a flat in Putney, where Enid ran an expanding but exhausting dressmaking business. Ada, in failing health, due largely to her enormous weight, was now being matched in size by her daughter, for Enid had begun to suffer from a glandular disease and was also becoming huge.

Although he greatly enjoyed teaching – and was beginning to enjoy the company of young children – Knight was having a difficult time. Entirely dependent on his salary, yet anxious to live as hectic a life as he had briefly enjoyed in the States, he found his limited means a constant frustration. He did not want to humiliate himself by begging his Uncle Robert for money, nor did he think he would actually be given any if he did ask. His salary as a very junior schoolmaster was minuscule, yet he wanted to hit the high spots of London as quickly – and as extensively – as he could. To this end, Knight had one important asset: his years on the *Worcester* had provided him with some good social contacts who would invite him to parties. These contacts kept him going from 1918 until 1924 – a considerable period of time in which to maintain a double life by concealing his modest home with the two fat ladies at Putney, hinting at Tythegston as his socially acceptable background and living a playboy life on the cheap.

It was, of course, a worrying hand-to-mouth existence and Knight found it increasingly hard to conceal the strain. His social acceptance, however, was never in question, for he was tall and handsome – a 'deb's delight' – and had developed an easy line in the social patter of the times.

At home in Putney, Knight's enthusiasm for animals held full sway. There were white mice in the living-room, grass snakes in the bath, a parrot in the kitchen and a couple of ferrets in the garden. All these creatures held a special place in Knight's affection. Although at this stage most of his considerable talents were used in maintaining a busy social life, his gift for making animals respond to him and show him complete trust never diminished.

As the years passed Knight became dissatisfied. He enjoyed teaching but the social round gradually became irksome and pointless. He continued to read Buchan and other adventure stories and retained a highly romantic notion of becoming an adventurer. Increasingly he saw himself in this role – but where could he go and what could he do? Should he join an expedition somewhere or try to go back to the navy? The former was attractive but unattainable, the latter redolent of rules, regulations and buckling down – and just what his Uncle Robert would have liked.

Knight's craving for romantic adventure – even his vision of the First World War as a combination of romantic heroism and glamorized duty – is epitomized by a passage in Buchan's *Greenmantle*, a book to which Knight was greatly attached:

> For more than a year I had been a busy battalion officer, with no other thought than to hammer a lot of raw stuff into good soldiers. I had succeeded pretty well and there was no prouder man on earth than Richard Hannay when he took his Lennox Highlanders over the parapets on that glorious and bloody 25th day of September.

But, for various reasons, Hannay's thoughts took a new turn and he considered that 'there might be other things in the war than straightforward fighting.'

This key phrase may have returned to Knight's mind when he went, in April 1925, to what might have been just another dinner party. For him, this was to be a major turning-point, as one of the guests was Vernon Kell. He discreetly asked Knight if he would come to see him at his office the next day. Knight did as he was requested – and to his astonishment found himself being asked to join M.I.5. It was to be the first of many meetings between the two men and it opened a door into a completely new world for the restless and unfulfilled Knight.

Kell was a brilliant linguist with great intuition (later described by an anonymous colleague as being able to 'smell a spy like a terrier smells a rat'). His father, Major Waldegrave Kell, was a regular army officer, and his mother was the refugee daughter of a Polish aristocrat. Fluent in Polish, French, Italian, Russian and German, Vernon Kell had served as an army officer in China during the Boxer rebellion but returned to England with bad dysentery and chronic asthma which dogged him for the rest of his life. After a brief spell with the C.I.D. secretariat, he became Director of the Home Section of the Secret Service

Bureau, responsible for investigating and preventing espionage throughout the United Kingdom. Kell's department, officially controlled by the War Office and working on a ludicrously small budget, was entitled M.O.5 until 1916, when it became the more independent M.I.5, answerable to the Secretary of State for War, with direct access to the Prime Minister. Despite these high-powered channels of communication, M.I.5's officers remained low-paid and publicly unacknowledged and unrewarded. The police made their arrests for them, thus giving the impression they had been responsible for the investigations.

Like Knight, Kell had been impressed by John Buchan's spirited patriotism. *Greenmantle* had been published in 1916; the following year Buchan was appointed Director of Intelligence at the Ministry of Information, which meant he was Press Liaison Officer for M.I.5 – a delicate position which had been engineered for him by Kell.

After the war, German and Soviet infiltration into the country became an increasing problem and Kell began to look round for more recruits who could be trained in specialist fields. Knight appeared to have all the qualities that Kell considered most important for an M.I.5 officer. He was intensely patriotic, highly versatile and bore himself with all the trappings of a country gentleman who not only hunted, shot and fished but was a witty and popular socialite. His naval training on the *Worcester* and his brief year at sea were also considered to be great advantages. Kell made no investigation into Knight's background and therefore knew nothing about the two ladies of Putney and the menagerie that occupied their modest home. This was typical of how M.I.5 was run under Kell's successors. Potential recruits who seemed 'good chaps' were employed at face value; hence such major mistakes as the employment of Burgess, Maclean, Philby and Blunt – amongst others.

When he had recovered from his astonishment, Knight's reaction to the invitation was ecstatic. M.I.5 represented to him all he could dream of in terms of romantic excitement.

Knight's new career did not interfere with his social life. A fast set of young people with aristocratic connections was considered to be an excellent milieu for a member of M.I.5, and in fact it was through this set that Knight had been introduced to Kell. After the war, night-clubs had sprung up all over London, many of them designed to evade the limitations of the new licensing laws. Knight and his friends frequented the cellar clubs of Soho and Leicester Square as well as the more fashionable ones of Bond Street and Piccadilly. There they enjoyed the music of the new American composers – Cole Porter, Irving Berlin, Gershwin and Kern – and the new dances such as the shimmy, the jog trot and the Charleston. After his American introduction to jazz, Knight had become an accomplished saxophonist and he loved going to the more sleazy clubs where good jazz was played – particularly his favourite, the blues – and young aristocrats mixed with prostitutes, pimps and drug-pushers.

It was against this background of somewhat frenetic gaiety that Knight first met Gwladys Poole. They were both fringe members of the Bright Young Things of the early twenties, many of them with private incomes and doting parents. Hoaxes, treasure hunts and dotty private language abounded, while attitudes towards sexual morality had become much more liberal. Wives and mistresses were not kept in the separate worlds of the Edwardian age and Soho and other red-light districts were no longer the only places in which to look for sex, except for homosexual sex. The 'new' girls were bubbling with fun, no longer had such strong taboos about sexual intercourse and had developed a line in sexual teasing. They exposed their knees and were humourosly sensuous. Fast driving in sports cars with the wind in their hair was the order of the day, and there were the new flying machines for even more sophisticated thrills. Far more athletic than their predecessors, girls had become 'good chaps' like boys, while still retaining their femininity.

Gwladys Poole, who came from a wealthy Somerset family, rode to hounds at every opportunity, loved fast cars and, although she was living in London, yearned for the countryside and its pursuits. She was deeply attracted to Knight because of his good looks and charm, as well as his interest in jazz and nature, and they had a whirlwind courtship. On his part, Knight needed marriage for security, for companionship and because M.I.5 preferred to see their employees happily married to the right class of person. They decided not to have sexual intercourse before their marriage.

In his first year with M.I.5, while still earning a relatively small income, Knight slowly learnt the background to Kell's creation. He discovered that the department had grown quickly, and had been the object of the jealousy of high officials who thought that all intelligence networks should be housed together. One merger, with S.I.S. (Secret Intelligence Service – M.I.6) had been mooted as an economy measure by Churchill when he was Secretary of State for War. This scheme was resurrected periodically between 1915 and 1927 but was never carried out. Kell was fiercely proud of his infant M.I.5, despite the lack of funds, and he had no intention of having its progress halted by a merger.

When Knight joined, the atmosphere was considerably more serious than it had been in earlier days, when even amateur dramatics had been permitted. At the end of the war, for instance, a satirical revue was mounted by M.I.5 personnel in which Kell himself was parodied, with his asthmatic cough, stooping walk and habit of settling his glasses far up on his forehead. But the gang-show image disappeared when an announcement was made in the *London Gazette* in 1924 that Kell and his deputy, Holt-Wilson, had 'retired'. In future they were to act in obscurity, and Kell, always known to Knight and his colleagues as 'the Colonel', never emerged in public in a professional capacity again.

Almost at the moment of Knight's arrival at M.I.5, Kell, Guy Liddell (then working at Scotland Yard as a counter-intelligence officer and later to join M.I.5) and other experts were involved in making virulent assertions that the Zinoviev letter was genuine. This letter, alleged to be a secret instruction from the Comintern to the Communist Party of Great Britain, was published in *The Times* and the *Daily Mail* on 25 October 1924 – a move that was to ensure the defeat of the Labour government, headed by Ramsay MacDonald, at the forthcoming general election. MacDonald, who had recently been negotiating a Russian treaty, was advised by M.I.5, among others, that the letter, alleging the existence of Communist cells in British army units which would paralyse military operations in the event of war, was absolutely genuine and that there was no question of the document being forged. The instruction had come into the hands of M.I.5, but publication was urged by Sir Reginald Hall, Unionist M.P. for Eastbourne and an ex-director of Naval Intelligence, who was tipped off that the MacDonald government was trying to suppress evidence of an important Soviet plot because of the nearness of the general election.

The letter is now considered to be a fake, inspired by Russian exiles and forged in Berlin, but its publication lost the Labour Party the election, aborted the Communists' intention of using that party as an umbrella, and convinced Knight of the danger of Communist subversion.

The next year, in 1925, two other momentous events occurred in Knight's life, virtually at the same time. A few hours before his marriage to Gwladys Poole his mother died of a heart attack. Anxious that the marriage should not be delayed, Knight decided to go ahead with the ceremony, organizing his mother's funeral at the same time. Enid was shocked; Cecil Kaye, Knight's cousin and childhood friend (at that time very close to Enid), corroborated: 'She very much disapproved of Max marrying Gwladys whilst the funeral arrangements were being made.' But it is not clear whether this was the only reason why Enid disapproved.

The marriage, from its inception at such an inauspicious moment, was a complete disaster. Knight was unable to consummate it. Gwladys decided to live in hope, praying that his lack of sexual drive would somehow come right. For a while they lived in some happiness in a flat in Sloane Street, largely bought with Gwladys's money. They continued their active social life and Gwladys still admired Knight's many talents, though she longed for the ordinary sexual passion that was so lacking. It was not long, however, before it became clear to her that her husband – gallant and romantic in every way, affectionate and handsome – had not the slightest interest in her body. It was an appalling shock and a real blow to Gwladys's self-confidence. To make matters worse, and presumably to boost his own ego, Knight continually flirted with other women. Their admiration of him – and his attraction to them – only served to strengthen Gwladys's feelings of inadequacy and rejection.

On his marriage, Knight's menagerie of white mice, grass snakes, live insects and the parrot, to say nothing of the ferrets, was moved from Putney, where Enid was still living, to Sloane Street. The move was greeted with mixed feelings by Gwladys who, at twenty-five, had not expected to become a zoo-keeper in addition to her other troubles. Nevertheless she respected his love for these animals and their strange, trusting response to him.

In 1927 Kell strengthened his position by bringing Guy Liddell into the department. It was he who was responsible for training Knight into a recognition of the political extremists in the Communist Party of Great Britain, knowledge that Liddell had built up at Scotland Yard and which Knight was to use with such insight in his first big case in the thirties. Married to Calypso Baring, one of Lord Revelstoke's daughters, Liddell had the aristocratic connections that were so typical of the department and he worked directly under Brigadier A. W. A. Harker, a distinguished ex-soldier who was now the Director of B Division.

Gradually, Kell was consolidating his position and forging

strong links with Scotland Yard (whose Special Branch would undertake all arrests for M.I.5), British colonies and dominions and other intelligence agencies abroad. When Kell had first been briefed for his new job by Colonel James Edmonds he had been told that as the work was secret there would be no public recognition of it, but 'it could be a job of vital importance to the country'. This it certainly was, and the lack of public glory was more than compensated for by the excitement of an unpredictable day-to-day life. Off-duty, Kell played croquet and fished, while during his working hours he employed criminals as informers, as well as a team of professional forgers, conveniently inhabiting cells in Parkhurst Prison.

This was the atmosphere into which Knight was plunged – a gentlemanly but ruthless intelligence service where intuition and painstaking research worked hand-in-glove. Knight took to it at once and Kell realized he had recruited a very able man. Indeed, Knight had all the correct characteristics for work in M.I.5. Like Kell, he had considerable intuition, strong powers of leadership, considerable personal charm and excellent administrative abilities. In addition, he had the natural flair for analysis essential to the intricate detective work so important in M.I.5's operations. Knight also had a love of the clandestine which was to be his strength as well as his undoing.

By the end of 1927 the Knights' sexual relationship had not improved, and because of their worry about this the social round in London was losing its appeal. Gwladys, now homesick for her own people, suggested she should move back home, but Knight, still anxious to keep the marriage intact, proposed another plan. Suppose they bought a pub devoted to country pursuits somewhere in the Somerset area? Gwladys could run it, while he would stay in the Sloane Street flat during the week and come down at weekends. They would live the lives of the country gentry and make some money out of them at the same time. Knight was genuinely fond of Gwladys and did not wish to lose her. Moreover, a separation would not be looked on kindly by Kell, who was a deeply religious man. Knight's M.I.5 salary was poor, so the property would have to be bought by Gwladys, but she could take up her interest in hunting again, while Knight could enjoy more leisurely pursuits such as fishing, surrounded, as he had been at Tythegston, by his beloved wildlife.

The arrangement hardly solved the central problem, but perhaps Gwladys felt that a more settled, less frenetic life might help, despite the fact that they would be together only at weekends. The plan was put into operation and, after a search, the Knights acquired the Royal Oak at Withypool on the edge of Exmoor. At that time it was a simple country inn with ten bedrooms, two bathrooms and a stone-flagged, sparsely furnished, public bar. Knight, who soon became a superb fly fisherman, acquired eight miles of fishing on the River Barle, which flowed through Withypool. Gwladys supervised all the cooking and the running of the hotel.

Tall, attractive and auburn-haired, Gwladys Knight was a vivacious woman with a passion for hunting and dogs. Being back on Exmoor and among her own friends temporarily eased the pain of what she felt to be a rejection of her own sexuality, and she led the country life to the full. But her mother, in whom she confided, was highly critical of Knight and anxious that the marriage should be dissolved. Gwladys still loved him deeply and her defence of him led to a rift between Gwladys and her mother, a rift that was to grow as wide as the increasing distance between Knight and herself. As soon as the Knights took on the Royal Oak they began to drift apart. 'They led separate lives even over the weekend,' remembers Colonel Robin Stable, who spent many of his leaves from the Indian Army at the pub. Knight, using his talents as an expert fly fisherman, was always out with fellow fishing enthusiasts, while Gwladys rode to hounds with a set of friends that were never to become Knight's.

It was a strange existence, for to all intents and purposes the Knights appeared to be an ordinary upper-middle-class, sporty young couple who, for a bit of a lark, were running a pub for decent folk who enjoyed hunting, shooting, fishing and good food. Most of the guests were known personally to Max and Gwladys and there was a warm, friendly atmosphere.

David Lloyd, later to become a long-standing friend of Knight's, vividly remembers this period when he, a withdrawn, unsporting fourteen-year-old, came to the Royal Oak for the first time in 1930 for a holiday. His mother had decided to take him and his half-sister, then aged eight, for an Easter holiday on Exmoor, the final ten days being spent at Withypool. Lloyd's father had been killed in 1916. For the expedition his mother had bought him a rod and tackle, which neither of them knew how to use. He soon got to know Gwladys and found her an exhilirating character.

'She owned a large, slobbery and strong-smelling bulldog called Fatty and a Hotchkiss-engined bull-nosed Morris named Chancy which she drove at ferocious speed on the then unmade Exmoor roads,' he remembers. 'Max was of course working in London, but on Friday evening he arrived and on Saturday morning I met him. We were total strangers and his weekends were doubtless precious to him, but that same day he took me, having vetted my new equipment, with one or two male guests, up to Lanacre Bridge and taught me the elements of fly fishing. He kept his eye on me throughout the day to the detriment of his own activities, and continued to do so for the rest of that weekend and the next one as well.' Lloyd stayed at the Royal Oak every summer for the next four years or so, and the pattern was always the same. He went with Knight on day-long fishing expeditions down the Barle, to Newland Ponds nearby, or to the canal at Sampford Peverell to fish for pike.

Knight also took Lloyd's young sister hunting for lizards in the stone walls down by the Barle; and he talked to them both for hours about everything 'except his mysterious job, which he described as "something between the War Office and Scotland Yard"'. David Lloyd looks back on his days at Withypool as little short of idyllic and the characters that surrounded Knight and Gwladys as very much larger than life. There was Tony Brunner, a wild, good-looking offspring of the Brunner-Mond family; Hugh Hamilton, a young racing motorist who was soon to be killed; Isaac (Ikey) Bell, a famous hunting character; and many more. Once Gwladys organized a treasure hunt all over Exmoor at night and this was one of Lloyd's most memorable experiences. He also recalls terrifying dashes over the country-side when Gwladys used to drive the cook home to her remote village at immense speed in the dark in the Morris, 'with the bulldog snorting and salivating in the back and the cook holding on for dear life'.

At this time the pub was festooned with rods and dank with drying waders and hunting clothes. A lounge bar was built out of an old cellar between the drawing-room and the public bar, with a hatch leading to the latter, through which on one occasion 'Colonel Stable and the one-armed Ned Lloyd, then field master of the Devon and Somerset Staghounds, dived with fearless aplomb.'

Lloyd sums up his experiences joyously: 'It was all enormous fun. Such trout as one did catch were cooked for breakfast split and fried in oatmeal and tasted as nothing ever has since.'

But despite the high jinks, the strain on Gwladys was increasing and Lloyd was to recall that sometimes she would begin an enthusiastic sentence – and then it faded away. A curious incident occurred during one of Lloyd's expeditions with Knight and made such an impression on him that he can still recall it with startling clarity.

'One day, as we wandered down the river bank, we came across a heron who had become impaled on some barbed wire and had died of strangulation. Max seemed fascinated and he spoke to me very analytically, very precisely about the bird's death. He said that nature was a ghastly, wicked war. He then took a photograph.'

In assessing Knight's personality, Lloyd, now a retired barrister, said: 'He was the archetypal Englishman of the times, deeply patriotic and with all the prejudices you would expect. But he bore his prejudices lightly. I look back on the time I spent with him as a golden age.' One could not describe Lloyd as an emotional man, but there were tears in his eyes as he spoke.

24

Colonel Robin Stable, who still lives at Withypool, gives a somewhat different picture of Lloyd's 'archetypal Englishman'. He remembers that 'Max kept telling us he worked for M.I.5 and brought secrets home to work on in the attic above the pub. Of course, no one believed him.' He also recalls that 'Max used to poach on other people's water, hiding the salmon in his trousers after he had laid down night lines.' The poaching was a new aspect to Knight's character, and hardly the kind of activity that should be indulged in by a gentleman. Yet in Buchan's *John Macnab*, poaching seems permissible for some gentlemen and perhaps Knight shared this view.

Sometimes Knight behaved very naively. Colonel Stable remembers an occasion in 1933 when Knight discovered that the Home Secretary was coming down to see some friends in Withypool. He found out what time the Home Secretary was returning to London on the Sunday evening and then decided he would attempt to share his carriage and see if he could get into conversation with him. At first Knight tried to persuade Colonel Stable to bribe the guard, but, understandably, he refused. He did, however, agree to find out from the station-master exactly which carriage the Home Secretary would be travelling in. Then, just as the train was about to draw out, Knight dashed up with a heavy suitcase, and threw himself into the Home Secretary's compartment. But he confronted that august personage for only a few seconds before being asked to leave by a bodyguard.

This curious episode illustrates Knight's desire to show off, to compensate for his lowly position in M.I.5 and for the hollow life that he knew he was living with Gwladys, a life that was now so surrounded by people and sandwiched between so many absences that there was no time to talk about their relationship. If this left Knight with feelings of guilt and inadequacy, then it must have left Gwladys with acute feelings of despair. She continued to love Knight and longed for his return from London each weekend, but he would soon go fishing with his cronies while she rode grimly to hounds.

In London, Knight continued to flirt with women while

managing to avoid their beds. Colonel Stable sometimes went to the flat in Sloane Street and remembers that 'he shared a common living-room with another chap next door. There was a case of grass snakes on the table which agitated the other chap very much indeed.'

Matters at M.I.5 proceeded slowly, so slowly that the excitement was beginning to drain away. By the end of the twenties, however, things started improving as Harker and Liddell began to groom Knight for his new work as a case officer, that is, a staff member of M.I.5 who recruits and controls agents. In selecting him for this position, Kell had seized on two of his obvious assets: his intuition and his many interests, all of which would help him build successful cover stories for his agents. A background of Mitcham, Tythegston, the *Worcester*, Putney, school-mastering, natural history, an unconsummated marriage and a pub on Exmoor, had not necessarily given Knight the kind of foundation required for masterminding such operations. He would require considerable training and experience before he could be considered of real value, and his youth and impatient ambition made him resent this slow process. He would need to possess exceptional judgement to find and direct people capable of the effective penetration of selected organizations. He would also need to know how to control their work and assess the content of the material they reported back. But Harker and Liddell shared Kell's view that Knight was worth training and there is little doubt that he was a quick and adept pupil. The training and waiting continued and it was not until 1930 that Knight was able to make a real mark, when he was put in charge of placing agents within the Communist Party of Great Britain (C.P.G.B.).

Communist spying in Great Britain had been given boost in 1921, when Ramsay MacDonald's Labour Government agreed that Russia should be allowed to establish a permanent representative in London. In 1927 there was a major prosecution at the Old Bailey when Wilfred Macartney and Georg Hansen were convicted of attempting to obtain information concerning the R.A.F. and the army. They also faced various other charges under the Official Secrets Act. Harker from M.I.5 and Liddell from his former position in Scotland Yard had engineered the investigation, which had resulted in a massive police raid and an armed search of the Soviet Trade Delegation, an act which had caused considerable Russian and British diplomatic agitation, resulting in the temporary severance of diplomatic relations with Moscow. This was an important victory for M.I.5, and government confidence in its abilities increased, for correspondence seized from the strong room of the Delegation gave alarming evidence of Soviet penetration into the trades unions, as well as the armed services. They also discovered that the Comintern were anxious to recruit ideological traitors rather than relying on those who were solely interested in money.

The first step in Knight's plan for full penetration of the Communist Party was to arrange for the tapping of telephones at the C.P.G.B. offices in King Street, London. Working from the new M.I.5 headquarters in the Cromwell Road, he also organized the vetting of Communist Party members who were employed in sensitive areas of British industry. This operation led to a number of workers being sacked, including a man named Percy Glading, who was known to have attended the Communist International in India in 1925 and had been involved in the Meerut conspiracy in which fifty-six Bolshevist agitators, led by a Comintern agent named Manandranath, were arrested in India. But there was not enough evidence against Glading to justify his own arrest. Nevertheless a file was opened on him at Scotland Yard and he was traced to Woolwich Arsenal, where he was employed in the role of examiner in the Navy Department, which handled a large quantity of plans and equipment on the secret list. Glading was sacked in October 1928 and mysteriously disappeared, but he was to return and become the catalyst for Knight's first successful case.

Knight was deeply concerned about Communist infiltration and felt the only way of defining its strength was for M.I.5 to use an agent who could be accepted by the C.P.G.B. in a

27

position of trust over a very long period. He believed that results would not be obtained for a considerable length of time, but when they did come, they might be explosive.

Liddell was impressed by Knight's arguments and finally convinced Kell that he should let his dynamic protégé have his way. Knight was overjoyed to be coming to grips with something important at last but he realized that it was absolutely essential to select the right agent. There was no obvious candidate immediately available to undertake such a difficult and dangerous task, someone unobtrusive and apparently loyal who would, above all, keep a cool head. It suddenly occurred to him that the qualities he sought might be found more easily in a woman than in a man. Knight began the search.

CHAPTER THREE

OLGA AND GWLADYS: 1930–1935

IN 1925 the Special Branch had raided the Communist Party headquarters in King Street, as well as the offices of the Young Communist League in Great Ormond Street. This exercise had been followed by the spectacular trial of ten members of the Party's executive committee, plus two other C.P.G.B. members, at the Old Bailey in November 1925. The charge against the twelve – who included Harry Pollitt, later to become General Secretary of the C.P.G.B. – was seditious conspiracy and incitement to mutiny. Five were sentenced to twelve months' imprisonment each and the other seven to six months, entirely because they refused to be bound over. But this result, after a six-year vigil by the Special Branch, could scarcely be regarded as very successful, particularly as no evidence had been produced to show that the C.P.G.B. was heavily financed by Moscow. In 1930 Liddell therefore briefed Knight to make the penetration of King Street much more effective by using his proposed woman agent. This was the first time Knight had been asked to prove himself, and he was determined to succeed.

At about this time Percy Glading, who had been attending the Lenin School in Moscow, reappeared in Britain and was the first person to come under surveillance. In Moscow, Glading had ostensibly studied Marxist philosophy and trade union structure. But while he was studying Glading had been quickly recruited and willingly learned the rudiments of espionage, involving the photographing of plans and books as well as a working knowledge of guns and ammunition. He was also taught how to organize a spy cell and use codes and ciphers. After a year in Moscow, Glading had become a fully fledged Communist agent.

Meanwhile, Knight had at last discovered a possible agent for infiltration into the C.P.G.B. Still in her twenties when Knight recruited her, Olga Gray[1] was temperamentally well suited to work of this kind. She needed excitement as well as a sense of belonging, even if that belonging was wholly based on deceit. She possessed a photographic memory and a strong, dominant personality that was entirely convincing with its consistent show of commitment and loyalty. She was also headstrong and highly insecure.

Olga was born in 1906, the eldest daughter of Charles Gray, who was a night editor of the *Daily Mail* in Manchester. Charles was himself a dominating character and inevitably he clashed with his daughter. Now, at the age of seventy-eight, Olga remembers that she often 'wished him dead'. She also remembers herself as a 'nasty child' but, in embittered old age, she cannot be a fair judge of her personality as a child. Her sisters, Marjorie and Joan, remember her as 'wilful' rather than 'nasty' and that is probably a more objective assessment. The fact is that Charles and Olga were too close in personality to have a peaceful relationship, and Charles, who was killed at Ypres in 1915, died too early in her life for them to discover any affection for each other.

The family was tinged with tragedy, the earliest example being the death of Olga's eldest brother, Edward, who died of meningitis at the age of five, after a fall at a local fair. Charles, who had taken him there, never forgave himself for his beloved

---

[1] It had been assumed by historians that Olga Gray was dead, but I managed to track her down in Canada through contacts of Sir Eric St. Johnston, former Chief Commissioner of the Metropolitan Police and an old friend of Knight's. At first, frightened of either Communist or M.I.5 retribution, she refused to see me, but, after much persuasion and reassurance, eventually agreed. Now in her late seventies, and living in a suburb of Toronto, Olga gave me a long interview on which this text is based.

child's death. Years later, Victor, the fourth child, was knocked off his bicycle and killed by a car when he was seventeen, a further blow that made Elizabeth, their mother, more dependent on Olga. Not that Elizabeth was a weak personality: she was as strong, if less volatile, as her husband and eldest daughter.

After her father's death, Olga quickly assumed the role of head of the family, only just managing not to dominate Elizabeth whom she loved as the sheet anchor of her life. As well as her two sisters she had two surviving brothers: Richard (who was later to become Olga's bodyguard and a distinguished policeman) and John, who was born shortly after Charles's death. Physically as well as emotionally strong, Olga used her natural powers of leadership in both ways. She was fiercely protective of the younger children, but often bullied them.

At eleven Olga and her sisters were sent to boarding school, first at St. Katharine's, Wantage, and later at St. Dunstans, Plymouth, where they were taught by an Anglican order of nuns. Olga's interest in literature flourished. She also excelled at games and at school was much the same as she was at home, a tom-boy with a wilful nature, a hot temper and an increasing sense of insecurity. Within her family 'she found herself closer to the boys', Richard and John, rather than Marjorie and Joan, accusing them of being like 'Bubbles' in the Millais painting, and they were certainly very pretty. Although Olga herself was a very striking girl she was not pretty, another factor that contributed to her self-doubt. Captain of hockey and netball at St. Dunstans, Olga continued her somewhat aggressive path, becoming more outspoken, more intolerant and alternately more protective and bullying. At the same time she became increasingly convinced that she was ugly, and therefore sexually unattractive.

Her mother, impoverished and distraught at Victor's untimely death, took in lodgers to meet the school fees and took up Conservative canvassing to distract her from obsessive thoughts of Victor. A friend of Mrs. Neville Chamberlain, she was encouraged to take on the running of a youth club in Smethwick, in which all the family participated.

Olga left school at seventeen and took a secretarial job with the A.A. At the club she met a young woman called Dolly Pyle. Dolly was a secretary at M.I.5 and Knight had asked her to look out for possible recruits. Olga's restless, obviously unfulfilled personality caught her professional eye. Despite Olga's domineering ways it was clear to anyone of perception that she was insecure, had a poor image of herself, and was ripe for development, and Dolly knew that Knight wanted a woman whom he could mould.

In the summer of 1928, when Olga was twenty-three, she was playing clock golf at a garden party in Edgbaston, at the home of the Conservative agent. There she again met Dolly Pyle who, over the cucumber sandwiches, blandly asked her if she would like to join the 'secret service'. Olga thought she was joking but eventually Dolly convinced her that she was serious and a very disconcerted Olga said she would be interested. She heard nothing more for two years, until she was twenty-five, an age at which she had sworn she would be married. Instead she was summoned to London and met at Euston by Knight. She arrived on a Saturday and, incredibly, by Monday she was a voluntary worker at the office of the Friends of the Soviet Union.

Directly Knight met Olga he knew that Dolly Pyle had been right. Here was a spirited but malleable young middle-class woman, who was intellectually and academically bright, and in need of an occupation. She was just the kind of person he needed to infiltrate the Communist Party. With no ties in London, no male friends to confide in, a staunch Tory background and a façade of leadership, she would be ideal to go 'red', i.e. to convince the Communists that she had seen the intellectual and political light. Knight also knew from Dolly Pyle – and from his conversations over the weekend with Olga – that she was the kind of person who would relish the excitement of plunging into a very different world from her own and appearing to be totally committed to it.

In 1983, reflecting on Knight's personality, Olga said: 'He was very charming, very avuncular, but I didn't have any sexual feeling for him, largely because I didn't see how he could possibly be attracted to me. It just seemed impossible because at the time I felt totally unfeminine.'

So, from the autumn of 1931 until 1937, doing a conventional secretarial job during the day, working voluntarily for the Friends of the Soviet Union at night and returning to her mother in Edgbaston over the weekends, Olga established the pattern of a highly intelligent, tough young woman who was becoming more and more sympathetic to Communism. At the Friends of the Soviet Union she typed letters, helped to bring out the newspaper, *War*, and went to various cell meetings. It was an exhausting, harrowing life, and towards the end of this period it was almost to break her.

'Oddly enough,' Olga remembers, 'the most terrifying ordeal of my life in the early thirties was a popular song that was continuously played on the radio and used to obsess me to such an extent that I thought everyone at the C.P. was looking at me with growing suspicion. It was called "Olga Polovsky – the Beautiful Spy".'

Knight, however, was more worried by her occasionally headstrong behaviour. Always a keen games player, she joined Ealing Ladies' Hockey Club, which both amused and infuriated him, for he was certain King Street would not be able to equate their Communist volunteer with such a bourgeois activity. But no comment was made.

In 1934 Elizabeth moved down to London to live with her daughter, which lessened Olga's travelling commitments but increased the pressure on her concerning the secrecy of her real work, which was something she never hinted at, even to her family. Nevertheless, she was quite relieved when Harry Pollitt, General Secretary of the C.P.G.B., asked her to undertake a 'job', and for the first time in three years Knight could see Olga's infiltration of King Street beginning to bear fruit.

'The previous evening,' Olga remembers, 'I'd been to the cinema with Max in Trafalgar Square. We came out down a long staircase and just as I was walking into the street a black cat crossed my path. The next evening Pollitt asked me to go to India on a mission.' Olga was to take with her a large sum of money, which she smuggled out in sanitary pads. Stopping off in Paris to change this from sterling into dollars, she then boarded a P. & O. liner. 'I suppose if they had sent anyone else from King Street they would have been very noticeable amongst the wealthy passengers on the liner, for most of the C.P. volunteers and staff were working class. Luckily I was classy enough to merge, and I told my family and anyone who was interested that I was going to visit an uncle in Bombay.'

Before Olga left, Knight gave her some invisible ink so that she could jot down the numbers of the original bank notes, but Olga had problems making the ink work. Eventually she managed to use some of it and memorized the numbers of the remaining notes. She finally arrived in Bombay, 'but not before I had received a proposal of marriage from a man on the liner because I was the only single girl travelling'. Once there, Olga went to the Taj Mahal Hotel to meet a contact Knight had described who turned out to be the conductor of the jazz band. He found a boarding-house for her to stay in and eventually she took the money to an address in the city. Problems arose when she was told that she had to take something back to England. She did not have the faintest idea what it was but she spent an agonizing three weeks waiting in Bombay and imagining that she was going to be arrested any moment. Then, suddenly, she was sent back empty-handed.

'This was the first time I had been really afraid,' she said, 'and suddenly I realized I wasn't playing spy games any longer.'

On her return from India, Pollitt asked Olga to work full time at the Party headquarters. Knight was delighted at her success and the confidence the C.P. had in her. At King Street she began to work for John Strachey, a former associate of Sir Oswald Mosley, and she saw a good deal of Knight, without becoming emotionally involved with him. His interest in the animal world still continued unabated and she remembers that he had bought a bullfinch and was teaching it to sing, much to her fascination as she watched his careful, patient work. She also saw Percy Glading regularly.

'He was a very nice man with a little daughter. I remember him being a very stimulating conversationalist and about the only person who could make an account of a film or play he'd seen absolutely riveting. I'll never forget how fascinating he made the plot of the *Ghost Train* sound.'

She also met the thriller writer John Dickson Carr, another C.P. worker, who, unbeknown to Olga, was also an M.I.5 agent, presumably directed by Knight. She was on very good terms with Harry Pollitt, who struck her as sincere and not particularly ambitious.

Then an old boy-friend of Olga's arrived in London and suddenly she could not tolerate the secrecy any longer. Feeling completely isolated and unable to respond genuinely to anyone, she eventually went to Knight and told him she could not carry on. Horrified at the prospect of losing such carefully established penetration, Knight begged her to reconsider, but she refused. Unfortunately, the pressure broke her and she was admitted to the National Hospital for Nervous Diseases in Queen's Square. Her sister Marjorie remembers this time vividly: 'I went to see her in a private ward there, to find the room literally full of flowers. They were everywhere but she was in a bad state. Of course I knew nothing yet I sensed, as I had before, she was no longer the staunch Tory of Gray family tradition.' As no-one else knew she was there, the flowers must presumably have come from Knight.

Losing such a talented agent was disastrous and Knight was determined to reawaken her sense of commitment and help her regain her confidence. While Olga was in hospital Knight went to see her every day. After a few weeks his persuasive techniques worked. Once again he had control of his agent and he was proving his worth as a case officer who was gaining both experience and confidence. Shaken, Olga emerged from hospital, gave up the boy-friend and returned to King Street.

During this time Knight decided to supplement his income by

writing thrillers, an occupation that was to increase his separation from Gwladys. His first attempt, *Crime Cargo*,[2] was a dire mixture of Dashiell Hammett and Mickey Spillane, tinged with John Buchan. Starring a bright young officer named Joycey, fresh from H.M.S. *Worcester*, the plot concerns some New York gangsters who try to take over the S.S. *Falkland*, a British ship chock-full of gallant sea-dogs, together with some wealthy American socialites who are taking a cruise with them. Dialogue among the gangsters is classic codswallop and much of the action is blood-thirsty.

> McGurk shrank back still further. It is probable that he only intended to make a show of defiance, or perhaps he only brandished his gun almost automatically. Even so, as he lifted his hand, Biretti was on him. The gang leader's knee drove home, and McGurk with a cry of agony rolled on the deck. Two soft-nosed bullets thudded home – one in the stomach and one through the lungs.
>
> McGurk raised himself up on his elbow, his pig-eyes already glazing, the breath whistling in his throat.
>
> 'Ye've got me – ye treacherous dago,' he gasped. Then he fell back, blood running from his mouth.
>
> 'Yeah, I've got you – Irish—' said Biretti quietly. There was a tense fearful silence after this, to be broken only by faint gurglings from Joe Holland, who was being violently sick.

Knight also tended to over-write his descriptive passages:

> Thus night fell, and the moon rose and shone down upon the sea and the S.S. *Falkland*. The evening before, the same moon had shed her light over the actors in this drama, touching one or another with her magic wand, and bidding romance come forth from her hiding-place. Now the moonlight seemed somehow cold and remorseless, the pale

[2] Published by Philip Allan (London, 1934).

36

beams appeared to spread an unearthly light around, making the calm sea look sinister by reason of its very calmness. The curtain of night had fallen on the stage, and none knew what scenes might be enacted on the morrow when the curtain rose once more with the coming of daybreak.

While Knight was writing in London, and at the same time manipulating an unwilling Olga Gray back into the C.P.G.B., Gwladys's loneliness was complete. Through pressure of work Knight rarely returned to the Royal Oak even at weekends and it was becoming clear that the marriage was now one in name only.

By 1934 Gwladys felt she could no longer cope alone with the hotel and the humiliation of desertion. Friends and customers had begun to notice her plight and their sympathy was unbearable. Deeply depressed, towards the end of that year she sold the pub and moved to Minehead where she took over a hairdressing and beauty salon. Sciatica added to her troubles and the barbiturates prescribed for its relief made her feel worse. On 16 November 1935, she travelled to London to stay at the Overseas League Club in St. James's. She was in a mood of considerable despair, despite the fact that she had written a cheerful note to Knight on her arrival at the club. It read:

Sweetheart – Just arrived for a few days' shopping. Will you give me a ring in the morning to see what we can fix up – not too early, as I will be having breakfast in bed and will not be leaving here until after 10 a.m. Love, G.

On receipt of the note Knight rang the Overseas League Club and was told by the housekeeper that his wife was asleep. Impatiently, he rang again, and then again. By this time it was almost eleven and Knight told the housekeeper to go up and wake her. After what seemed an interminable delay the house-keeper reported that she could not be wakened.

37

Thoroughly alarmed, Knight took a taxi to the club and found Gwladys in a deep coma. Terrified, he called in a Harley Street doctor who arranged for her to be taken to a nursing home in Wilbraham Place. Gwladys still showed no sign of a return to consciousness and the doctor, Warner, sent for Sir William Wollic, a celebrated authority on poisons, and medical adviser to the Home Office. He arrived just after midnight on 17 November. With a frantic Knight in attendance, both doctors did what they could to save Gwladys's life, but she had taken a massive dose of barbiturates, backed up by aspirin. A few hours later pneumonia developed and she died.

Knight was devastated; his grief, as much as his guilt, was genuine. Gwladys's mother and brother (her father was now dead) were shocked, and their own grief was immediately channelled into hatred for Knight. They blamed him for the way he had neglected Gwladys, and for causing the rift between mother and daughter that had come about as a result of Gwladys's spirited defence of that very neglect. In addition, they were deeply concerned that Gwladys had left her considerable private fortune (£22,000) to Knight. In their misery the Pooles' grief turned to suspicion, and soon they had convinced themselves that Knight had either driven Gwladys to take her life or had actually murdered her. It is not easy to see how the latter could possibly have been done, but they were determined to have their revenge on him and accordingly briefed a well-known criminal counsel, Reginald Seaton, to represent them at the inquest.

The inquest, which was widely reported, plunged Knight into a scandal that was permanently to tarnish his reputation at M.I.5. Scandal was the last thing he needed at this stage of his career and his grief was tinged with fear.

Only formal evidence of identification was taken in the coroner's court at Hammersmith, before proceedings were adjourned to allow time for a chemical analysis to be obtained. Under cross-examination it soon became clear that husband and wife had not seen each other for some months. In reply to a statement from the coroner that Gwladys's health had been good Knight said:

'Yes, sir, until August of this year when she had an extremely acute attack of sciatica and on my advice and that of a friend, she went to Bath for a course of treatment. She was there for nearly three months, undergoing treatment under one of the best doctors in Bath.'

'I think you last saw her whilst down there?'

'Yes, sir.'

'Do you know the date?'

'It was about the first week in September, sir.'

The coroner then explained to Knight that he was prepared to sign a burial order but the inquest would be reopened after the necessary adjournment.

When the inquest was resumed a few days later, Dr. Roche Lynch, the Home Office analyst, stated that it was impossible to discover just how much poison Gwladys had swallowed, but it was certainly more than a medicinal dose. He thought that she must have taken either one single dose or a series of doses of barbiturics over a short period of time, together with a quantity of aspirin.

Questioned by Knight's counsel, Dr. Warner (the Harley Street doctor Knight had first called) declared there was a possibility that any patient who took as large a dose of barbituric drugs as Gwladys had would have woken up in a state of amnesia. He felt it likely that she might have mistaken the bottle containing the barbiturate for an aspirin bottle, as the pills were often the same shape and size.

Sir Bernard Spilsbury, a Home Office pathologist, thought the cause of death was quite clear in view of the symptoms: 'I have no doubt that the cause of death is coma, consequent on barbituric poisoning.'

Then it was Knight's turn to enter the witness-box. He was first asked to identify the letter from Gwladys which he had received on the Monday morning prior to her death. Knight's counsel then asked him whether Gwladys was 'casual in her habits as to where she put things'? Max replied that she was rather untidy.

'Would it be possible,' asked his counsel, 'that she put some barbituric pills in the aspirin bottle?'

'I would not say it was not consistent with what she might do,' replied Knight.

'You went through her belongings and you found no trace of any other bottle?'

Knight stated that he had not.

Later, Reginald Seaton, representing the Poole family, elicited from Knight (after objections from Knight's counsel regarding the admissibility of the question) the fact that Gwladys had possessed a substantial amount of money, but did not leave a will.

Seaton then asked Knight: 'Were you living apart from your wife, or were you cohabiting?'

Knight replied: 'Sometimes we were. It depended whether I went down to see her in the country.'

Knight went on to explain that he was living in London because of a serious breakdown in health which had affected his heart. He said that he had put Gwladys in charge of the Royal Oak, that he saw her frequently, and that she had moved to Minehead in 1934. (It was in fact true that Knight's heart had been marginally affected by a bout of scarlet fever, but this was not the reason for his desertion of Gwladys.) Asked whether he was supporting his wife, Knight replied that they were mutually contributing to each other.

Seaton then asked him: 'Did your wife's health start to deteriorate during the time she was managing the hotel at Withypool?'

'Not to my knowledge,' he replied. 'I never knew her to have any breakdown in health until August this year.'

Seaton's next question infuriated Knight: 'Did you give her mother an accurate description as to how your wife had died? You knew she had died from pneumonia.'

'I was not at all sure she had died from pneumonia,' replied Knight.

But Seaton pressed on. 'When you wrote to the mother, did you intimate to her, or was the general intimation to be drawn from your letter, that in fact your wife had been buried?'

Knight denied that he had written in this way, but Seaton was not to be fobbed off.

'Do you think you had been as frank as you might have been?'

'I think I was as frank as my wife would have wished,' said Knight, as his counsel attempted to come to his rescue by asking if the question was a proper one.

But Seaton simply replied coolly, 'What I was asking were questions in order to elucidate if this man was in any way responsible, not criminally, for his wife's death.'

In reply to further questions, Knight explained that his wife and her mother had been estranged for the last eight years.

In his summing up, the coroner said: 'Many of these cases are of people who take big doses of barbiturics and are cases of suicide, but many are accidental. There is obviously a doubt in a case like this as to which, so we have to express that doubt, and we have also to express it in the verdict. . . . The findings of this court will have to be an open verdict. Mrs. Knight died from poisoning by a barbituric hypnotic preparation, there being insufficient evidence to show in what circumstances her death occurred.'

Gwladys Knight was buried in the graveyard of the tiny windswept church at Hawkridge, a remote spot on Exmoor. The funeral was attended by a large number of mourners and wreaths were placed beside the grave, which was lined with bronze and yellow chrysanthemums. The card on the Pooles' wreath read: 'In loving remembrance of "Bunchie" from her mother and brother, Gordon.' The tension between the Pooles and Knight was obvious and, travelling back to London, he contemplated the extent of their hatred as well as the scale of his own guilt. He knew he had not wilfully set out to kill Gwladys, but by finally deserting her he had brought about her death just as surely. There was little doubt in his mind that she had committed suicide or accidentally overdosed in a muddled, desperate manner. What, one wonders, did others who knew the Knights make of this tragedy? David Lloyd, who had found such delight in the Knights' company at Withypool, reflects:

'There is no doubt that the strain of running the hotel almost single-handedly told on Gwladys, who seemed to resent the fact that Max escaped to London for the whole week. But I admired her enormously for her warmth, her dash and courage and her determination to see that her guests had fun, apart from good food and good beds, and I still often think of her.'

The fierce winter storms of Exmoor soon began to weather the inscription on the gravestone at Hawkridge; now it has almost disappeared.

CHAPTER FOUR

THE WOOLWICH ARSENAL SPY RING
1935–1938

WITH Gwladys's death and his own culpability on his mind, Knight plunged back into work at M.I.5 with renewed vigour and absorption. Both Kell and Liddell had been much concerned by the tone taken by the Pooles' counsel at the inquest, as well as the rumours that circulated for months afterwards, saying that Knight had murdered his wife and that his income had now been considerably increased by her fortune. Knight himself was only too aware of the damaging nature of the scandal and the persistent rumours. He must have wondered whether he was expendable or whether M.I.5 would consider him too valuable to lose. In the last analysis it was the successful infiltration of the C.P.G.B. by the reluctant Olga Gray that saved him.

Olga, however, almost removed Knight's last foothold by reasserting her independence and telling Harry Pollitt that she was resigning from the Communist Party 'because her boy-friend did not approve'. Two days later it was the Communists' turn to apply the pressure: Olga was approached by Glading, who wanted her to run a safe house. More or less at the same time, or so Olga now claims, her boy-friend left her and she decided to comply with Pollitt's pressure and help Percy Glading. Together Olga and Glading went shopping for furnishings for the new venture. 'The curtains are in my daughter's house now,' she remembered in 1983. Knight had already suggested an address to her – a ground-floor flat at 82 Holland Road, Kensington, which, as Glading had specified, did not have a porter. Olga suddenly realized that all her years of work were coming to a climax. She had no real idea of what Glading's plans were and she did not fully understand them until the eventual trial. But she was aware that as the weeks dragged by she had grown very fond of Glading.

This was a crucial time as far as Knight was concerned. He knew he had to wait until he was able to make a major, comprehensive swoop. One false move and the case would come to a premature, unsatisfactory conclusion with perhaps only half the Communist agents in the bag. From the wings, of course, it was not so hard for Knight to play a waiting game, but Olga, in the thick of a highly dangerous, indefinitely prolonged situation, was under enormous pressure.

Glading gave Olga cash with which to pay the rent (£100 a year, paid monthly in advance), and also told her to have three sets of keys made, of which he must have two. Soon Glading introduced her to a man known as Peters, describing him as an Austrian officer who had served in the Russian cavalry, risen to the rank of captain and then spent some time in an Austrian monastery. All this Olga reported faithfully back to Knight.

In May 1937 Glading suggested to Olga that she should have a holiday and that on her return she should take up a job. So far she was still undertaking ordinary secretarial jobs as well as running the flat.

'Percy said he would pay me £5 a week for additional work that he would give me – work that would be to do with photography. I said I knew nothing about using cameras but Percy told me not to worry – he would find someone to instruct me.'

In the meantime, Knight was able to identify Peters as Theodore Mely, a Soviet intelligence officer working for the N.K.V.D. He was to disappear when Stalin purged the service, but was quickly replaced by a Mr. and Mrs. Stevens.

'They were clearly foreigners,' Olga remembers, 'and they

spoke to each other in French. Percy told me that Mrs. Stevens was going to do some photographic work at the flat and that I was to help her.'

On 11 October a long refectory table was brought into 82 Holland Road and on 13 October a camera and photographic apparatus arrived. Over the next few days the Stevens tested out their equipment by photographing maps of the London underground railway and Olga was able to send a brief message to Knight which read:

October 11: photographic apparatus [listed] arrived. October 13: another meeting – G and a Mr. and Mrs. S who spoke French. October 18: Mr. and Mrs. S experimented 3½ hours, photographing maps of London underground. G very jumpy.

On 21 October Mrs. Stevens arrived in the early evening, clutching a large oblong parcel, which was clearly seen by Knight's observers outside. Olga could see that it was some kind of plan and Mrs. Stevens told her that she, her husband and Glading were going to photograph it with at least forty-two exposures. She could sense Mrs. Stevens was very nervous, so nervous that she told Olga to stay in the bedroom until the job was finished. Later, however, Olga emerged from her bedroom and saw that the plan had been photographed in sections and that the negatives had been left to be developed and dried off in the flat. She was then able to take notes of all the markings and serial numbers she could make out, for she knew that armed with these, Knight's experts could discover exactly what Percy and the Stevens had been photographing.

'It was all very tricky making notes of the markings on the plan becuase the negatives were hanging just above the bath. I had to get into it to find out the information,' remembers Olga.

Knight's observers watched Mrs. Stevens leave with the plan wrapped in newspaper. She took a taxi – which they followed – to Hyde Park Corner, where she met her husband and fifty-four-year-old George Whomack, a mechanical examiner who had worked at Woolwich Arsenal since 1918, to whom Mrs. Stevens gave the parcel. He had recently been promoted to assistant foreman and was considered by his employers to be a first-class worker. All three walked a short way down Piccadilly where they then split up. The Stevens, conscious of the need to cover their tracks, took the tube to Tottenham Court Road, a bus to Marble Arch and then, by a circuitous route, reached their flat in the Edgware Road. Whomack, meanwhile, caught the 5.11 train to Welling.

Thanks to Olga's detailed notes, the plan was quickly identified as that of a fourteen-inch naval gun of the newest type. There were three of these top secret plans in the Woolwich ordnance factory and, although access may well have been permitted to a number of people, Knight was fairly certain that it was Whomack who had taken the plan out and also returned it.

Knight was now able to put his department on full alert and the Stevens, Glading, Whomack and the house in Holland Road were under constant surveillance. But he did not want to move yet. The trap was not yet ready for springing, as he had a hunch that still more people could be heading for it.

Then, on 2 November 1937, Glading told Olga that the Stevens were having to return to Moscow because of the illness of their small daughter. He went on to tell her that there would probably not be any more work until after Christmas. In the meantime he suggested that they might practise with the photographic equipment. But after the Stevens (Knight now knew their real name was Brandes) left on 6 November, Glading came to the flat and took away the stand and later the camera. Olga and Knight therefore supposed that he was practising photography at his house in South Harrow.

On 12 January 1938, Glading told Olga that he had a special job to do at his home over the weekend of 15 and 16 January. He told her that he had to photograph a book about 200 pages long and that it was going to be a difficult task. Knight instantly redoubled his surveillance on the South Harrow house and on 15 January, Glading left his home at 2.40, returning at 5.55 with something that looked like a magazine wrapped in a folded newspaper. The next day, 16 January, he was seen taking away a similar parcel.

Glading was trailed to Charing Cross Station. On arrival he went down to the public lavatory and gave the parcel to a young man who was carrying an attaché case. Still being followed, they went to Lyons Corner House for a meal and then parted. The young man was tailed to his home in Plumstead and Knight later identified him as twenty-two-year-old Charles Munday, yet another employee of Woolwich Arsenal, this time an assistant chemist in the War Chemists Department.

All the while, Olga repeats, she had the impression Glading was expecting someone to arrive to replace Stevens. She also knew that money was running short. Then, on 20 January, Glading rang her to see if she would lunch with him the next day. He also told Olga to prepare the flat for something important. When she met him on 21 January in the bar of the Windsor Castle, he was carrying a suitcase. He told her to return to the flat by 6 p.m. as there was urgent photography to be done and he needed help. Finally, he said he had an appointment at Charing Cross at 8.15.

Acting on this information, Knight decided that the time for the denouement had come and that arrests would finally be made at Charing Cross Station. Glading was seen to be approached at 8.15 by a middle-aged man who was carrying a brown-paper parcel. Both were arrested, much to their amazement, and taken to Scotland Yard. The brown-paper package contained the blueprints of a pressure bar apparatus for testing detonators, showing the working detail. Glading's contact was Albert Williams, a carpenter at Woolwich Arsenal, once again a man with a reputation for being a conscientious, industrious worker.

Special Branch then raided Glading's home and a fascinating haul was discovered: a Leica camera, a Zodolette camera, a piece of paper containing part of an anti-tank pistol about the size of a pencil, and four spools of Leica film. On these spools were photographs of each of the 200 pages of the book Glading had photographed over the weekend of 15 and 16 January. The most important find was five photographic plates of quarter-plate size relating to a special kind of fuse that was used in a top secret anti-submarine bomb. The evidence against Glading was damning and also implicated Williams, as one of the five photographic plates showed a tiny strip of wallpaper identical to that in Williams's room, which had clearly been used as a studio and dark room. Clips were also shown in the photograph, as the plans were secured to a board, and these tallied exactly with others found in Williams's house.

Despite taking great care, Glading had slipped up while taking the photographs and left a fingerprint, a further piece of conclusive evidence discovered by Chief Detective Inspector S. S. Birch, second-in-command of Scotland Yard's fingerprint department. He described the coup in his own melodramatic words in an inaccurate newspaper article which appeared some months after the trial:

> While he was setting up his photographic equipment with the scupulous care that had made him a master spy, he used gloves and left no fingerprints on the glazed dishes, glass negatives, nor the polished surfaces of the enlargers and camera boxes. All set – he snapped a switch to test the two big arc lights. One bulb popped into darkness with a broken filament. George [Percy Glading], anxious to get to his appointment at Charing Cross Station, stripped off his glove, put back a replacement bulb, adjusted the green metal lampshade, nodded his satisfaction – and hurried out.
>
> Behind him – as I was to find under my powerful little pocket microscope that gives me an enlargement of six diameters – he had left the clear impression of his nasty fingers on the bulb, the green shade, the switch.
>
> It was useless now for him to protest ignorance of the photographic apparatus.

A few days later Munday and Whomack were arrested after a search had been made in the Holland Park flat. There a camera and stand were all set up and ready with some of Glading's fingerprints on the apparatus, as discovered by Birch. A further search was made of Williams's house and documents mentioning Munday's name were discovered. The case against the Woolwich Arsenal conspirators was complete and Knight had pulled off a much needed coup for himself and M.I.5.

Olga, known as 'Miss X', was the principal witness for the prosecution Her feelings were in turmoil as for the first time she was forced to face the reality of destroying a man who had become her friend, who had trusted her completely and who was deeply shocked to find that she was an M.I.5 agent. There was also the suffering of his wife and daughter to be taken into consideration.

Despite Knight's reassurances, Olga was terrified that her real identity would somehow be exposed in court, and indeed the defence barristers, Dudley Collard and Denis Pritt, were themselves Communist sympathizers. Fear of assassination after the trial was uppermost in her mind, particularly when, at the magistrates' hearing, she was handed a piece of paper with her real name and address on it and C. B. McClure, the prosecuting counsel, asked if they were accurate. Collard immediately said: 'I can see no reason why her name should not be disclosed if she is going to be the principal witness in this case. It is not a charge of blackmail, or anything of that sort.'

But to Olga's relief the magistrate ruled that her name should not be disclosed, pointing out that, as the case was obviously going for trial, the decision on what was to be held in camera should be deferred.

In his opening speech, McClure said: 'The case for the prosecution, which I have to describe, is a most serious one, that Glading during some months in last year and the final month of this year, if you accept the evidence, was a person prepared to act as a traitor to his country for gain to himself. Whether the other men were willing or not matters nothing – he succeeded at different times in persuading them to break their duty of allegiance to the Crown by which they were employed and to bring from the Arsenal documents of a confidential and secret nature that he, with the most elaborate apparatus which he had prepared, might take copies of them by means of photographs. . . . It is suggested that there is evidence of contact with a Foreign Power on the part quite clearly of Glading and the other with whom he was associating.'

One newspaper account revealed how tense Olga was: 'Miss X, who spoke with a cultured voice, then told her story. At one time she appeared distressed and Mr. McClure asked her if she would like to sit down. She replied that she would rather stand.'

The trial of Glading, Williams, Whomack and Munday began at the Old Bailey in March 1938 with Mr. Justice Hawke presiding. They all pleaded guilty to an indictment on five counts:

1. Glading and Whomack were charged with obtaining a plan of a naval gun.
2. Glading and Williams were charged with obtaining part of an anti-tank mine pistol.
3. Glading and Williams were charged with obtaining plans of an anti-submarine bomb fuse.
4. Glading and Munday were charged with obtaining information on explosives.
5. Glading and Williams were charged with obtaining plans calculated to be useful to an enemy.

The evidence against them, largely found in Glading's house, was substantial, even down to a diary reference. Reading from it, Mr. McClure said there appeared an entry '4.0 C.X.S.'. It was suggested that the initials stood for Charing Cross Station. Under the same date there was the entry '1.9.' with the letters 'C.M.' after it. Under 16 January was the entry '5 OCK' and under Friday 21 January – the date of the arrests – '8.20 C.X.'

The attaché case with a false bottom was also produced, but much of the evidence about the plans and armaments was given in camera, with police standing guard at the door.

Glading was described as 'an important personality in the British section of the Communist International'. Further facts as to his political activities were also revealed and later reported in the press, including details of his experiences in India. After his Indian adventure, the reports stated that Glading had devoted himself to industrial agitation in Britain, particularly among engineers. About this time, they claimed, Glading turned his mind towards the possibility of espionage, when he – for the second time – obtained a job as an engineer at Woolwich Arsenal, although he was dismissed for seditious activities in October 1928. Throughout 1932 he was concerned with the secret printing and distribution of the illegal Communist newspaper, the *Soldiers' Voice*, and a year later the C.P.G.B. put him in charge of a campaign for establishing Communist cells in factories in the East End of London. By the end of 1934 Glading had become one of the most important Communist agents in Britain, maintaining a link between the open Communist Party and the underground section responsible for espionage, sabotage, and seditious activity among the armed services.

On Monday 14 March sentences were given. Glading received six years, Williams four years, Whomack three years. Munday had been discharged at the beginning of the trial when the Attorney-General, Sir Donald Somerville, said he proposed to offer no evidence against him.

Passing sentence, Mr. Justice Hawke said: 'You were endeavouring to do anything you could to help some other country and injure this. This is your own country, but I cannot quite believe that that had any effect on your mind. I am satisfied that this was done for the sole and vulgar motive of obtaining money.'

But Hawke was wrong. Glading was clearly an ideological traitor. It was the others who wanted the money.

Of Miss X Hawke said: 'That young woman must be possessed of extraordinary courage. She has done a great service to her country. . . . I do not propose to call her into court to hear what I have to say, for reasons which I take it may be good reasons.'

Glading's face remained impassive as he heard the sentence but Williams was clearly shaken. Whomack, in public life a former deputy mayor and Bexley councillor, remained as inscrutable as Glading.

Because of the mystery surrounding Olga, both her background and the personality of Percy Glading were wildly dramatized, particularly in later newspaper articles by Chief Detective Inspector Birch:

The bravest girl I ever knew was a British secret agent. I met her the only time my duties at Scotland Yard's fingerprint department took me into that twilight world of international espionage just before the last war.

I shall always remember her. She had forgotten more about courage than many soldiers ever learn on the battlefield.

And the scene of the exploit which brought her to my notice? London, gay capital with its busy streets and carefree peacetime crowds. It was in this setting that Miss X, as I shall call her, trapped a gang of Russian spies.

Describing Miss X as 'a slender girl with dainty ankles and honey-blonde hair', he went on to write that she 'walked light-heartedly, seemingly unaware of discreet men in overcoats who stirred at street corners as she passed'.

Finally, Birch (or his Sunday newspaper editor) invented an aristocratic background for Miss X, a background that would increase the romance for the readers. The irony of the invention greatly amused Olga, for she was extremely poor, and realized that Knight would have no further use for her now that her cover was blown. 'To her mother and brothers in the old English manor house where she spent her childhood,' Birch wrote, 'she was an embarrassing pause in tea-time conversation – the daughter who "seemed to have got mixed up with some dreadful Communists in London".'

Carried away by his own dramatic prose, Birch described Glading as 'dark, distinguished, suave, with greying temples and good suits, a reader of poetry and a dreamer of revolt under high scarlet banners', overlooking the fact that in reality he was a short, rather clerical figure. Glading, just beginning his prison sentence, may have been grimly amused, for he had always had a good sense of humour.

The issue of *Time* magazine of 28 March, however, took a rather more urbane line:

> Sample of the tempting sort of bait successfully used to catch spies by His Majesty's Government has now been on view in London's ancient soot-blackened Bow Street Police Court for several weeks, officially tagged 'Miss X'. This slim, bobbed-hair blonde, English to judge from her accent, arrived curvesomely sheathed in clinging black, kept shifting her handsome fur piece with the sinuosity of Mae West, as she testified before a bug-eyed judge. 'She is a lady,' explained the Crown, refusing to divulge her name.

Directly after the trial, Knight asked Olga's brother Richard, a high-ranking policeman, to act as her bodyguard and despatched them to a quiet hotel in Berkshire to wait for things to blow over. Her sister Marjorie visited her there, and was struck by her sister's fear.

'She couldn't be on her own at all. Once I was there – and Richard was out – and I wanted to get some shopping in the village, but she begged me not to go. Then I read all the newspaper accounts and suddenly realized what my sister had done. It was incredible – I just couldn't believe it.'

Olga, having survived the days following the trial with a strange mixture of relief, anticlimax and fear of reprisal, was then paid off by Knight in a way that made her deeply bitter for the rest of her life. She had been paid fifty shillings a week for her M.I.5 work, and her secretarial jobs had also provided an income. Shortly after the end of the trial, she was taken out to lunch at the Ritz, not by Knight, but by an anonymous colonel. Duly congratulated and thanked for her loyal service, Olga was given a cheque for £500 as a completion fee.

After a spell as a high-powered secretary in industry, she met a Canadian air force man on the underground, married him and went to live in Canada. But her nerves never recovered from her ordeal and the rest of her life was marred by fear of retribution and frustration that her extraordinary talents, stretched to their limit in her relationship with Glading, should be left untapped for so many years.

But for Knight, the arrest and sentencing of Glading and his compatriots was a godsend, bringing him a sharp increase in respect from Kell, Harker and Liddell. The scandal surrounding the manner of Gwladys's death and the subsequent inquest was now overtaken by his successful breaking of the Woolwich Arsenal spy ring. Considerable information had been gathered concerning C.P.G.B. activities, as well as positive proof that Soviet Russia was subsidizing Communist parties in other parts of the world – the legacy of Olga's hazardous Indian trip.

Olga Gray's penetration of the C.P.G.B. won enormous plaudits for Knight and secured him a senior position in M.I.5. But Olga, now cast into the wilderness, had to make a new life for herself.

'I was a 50 shillings a week spy,' Olga told me. 'Then I was dumped. In those days the adrenalin really flowed but since then the excitement has never been rekindled. That's why I feel so restless – and my abilities remain so unfulfilled.'

1 Knight, aged sixteen, in the uniform of the merchant navy training ship,
H.M.S. *Worcester. (Private collection)*

2 Tythegston Court in Glamorgan, the home of Knight's aristocratic Welsh cousins, who regarded him as the black sheep of the family. *(Private collection)*

3 The Royal Oak at Withypool on Exmoor, a pub taken over by Knight and his first wife, Gwladys, in 1927. Knight had joined M.I.5 in 1925. *(Private collection)*

4 David Lloyd *(second left)* with Knight *(centre, smoking a cigarette)* on a fishing expedition by the banks of the Barle on Exmoor. *(Private collection)*

5 Gwladys *(first left)* on the steps of the Royal Oak with customers (who were probably friends too) shortly before she committed suicide in 1935. *(Private collection)*

6 Knight's range of interests and abilities was wide – as spy, naturalist, fisherman, cricketer and jazz-musician. The clarinet, as shown in this caricature, was one of his favourite instruments. *(Private collection)*

7 Knight was a keen fisherman, but did not always abide by the rules of the game. He was known to poach on other people's water, sometimes hiding salmon, which he caught on night lines, in his trousers. *(Private collection)*

CHAPTER FIVE

SPYING OUT THE LAND: 1935–1940

THE publication in 1934 of *Crime Cargo* had hardly taken the world by storm, but this did not deter Knight from writing another gangster saga called *Gunman's Holiday*, which Philip Allan published in 1935.

Gunman's Holiday begins in typical Max Knight style:

When 'Snowey' Polini heard the news that 'Bat' McGowan of New York was going to England on a vacation, he first of all spat into the silver cuspidor which stood on the antique side table near his magnificent four-poster bed, and then said slowly through his half-closed lips: 'All boloney!'

The same could be said of *Gunman's Holiday*, in which the warring Chicago gangs arrive in England – and later gravitate to Eastbourne – to continue their feud against a background of Hurlingham, cricket and the South Downs. The main characters include Sally, an English rose, the British-educated daughter of one of the gang leaders; Bruce (a Hannay stereotype), her Scottish boy-friend and a decent chap; and Valentino Polini, the fourteen-year-old son of the principal gangster. Jokes are aimed at all foreigners, especially those with funny-sounding names, none of whom can speak the language, play a straight bat or have the least notion of an Englishman's honour. Often they are greasy, running to fat and, in the case of Valentino, brutally ragged by little English chaps-in-the-making at their prep school.

Here he was discovered being held under the cold douche by a stocky, freckled lad, named Hudson, whose efforts to give Tino a bath while still in his natty fawn plus-four suit, were being applauded by several other boys who stood round, grinning, and offering light-hearted advice as only English schoolboys can. With a hoot of merriment the group of boys took up the cry: 'Vaselino! Good old Vaselino!' Others seized upon his surname and danced like toreadors shouting: 'Poloney! Poloney! Come and look at the walking hot dog!'

Much can be read into the character of Bruce, the hero of the book, who represents all the unspoken sexual virility that Knight may well have wanted. Bruce is a classic example of manhood, standing four-square against a background of love of the countryside, field sports, pugilistic abilities, honour, integrity, conservatism – a thoroughly decent fellow who would soon see off every Commie or Fascist agitator (or outlandish foreigner) who crossed his path. Bruce, a pseudo-Buchan figure, would have been tops in the secret service.

He was gazing at Sally McGowan with that peculiarly sheep-like expression which young men in love always adopt when regarding the object of their affections. The soulful look did not suit this particular young man, for he was of the type that appears more at home on a rugger field than anywhere else. Taller than average, with a fine pair of shoulders that seemed made for shoving in the front row, his face was of the rugged kind, not by any means handsome but essentially masculine. Grey eyes that looked straight at you, and a determined square jaw, gave Bruce Ferguson a distinction that almost fitted him for the companionship of the vision by his side.

This cliché-ridden description of heterosexuality represented nevertheless a comic-strip ideal that Knight had of himself – a far cry from his real feelings.

The dedication of *Gunman's Holiday* was to J. and D. W. –
Joan and Dennis Wheatley – whom Knight had met at a party.
Dennis Wheatley, the thriller writer and enthusiast for the
occult, who introduced Knight to the Great Beast, Aleister
Crowley, described the occasion vividly in his autobiography
Drink and Ink.[1]

> The place was packed with lovely, but mostly brainless
> young debutantes. Their conversation was solely about
> clothes, dances they were going to and their boy friends; so
> Joan and I were fish out of water. However, there was one
> other guest who was in the same situation: a tall beak-
> nosed man in his late thirties, whose name was Maxwell
> Knight. The three of us settled down in a corner to talk and
> it transpired that, like myself, he had been a cadet on
> H.M.S. *Worcester*.

From this chance meeting a friendship grew that was to alter
the lives of the Wheatleys, as well as Dennis's step-children,
Diana and Bill Younger. Wheatley encouraged Knight in his
writing and helped him to publicize *Gunman's Holiday*, and
soon they were all on very good terms. Knight liked the gregari-
ous Wheatley for his vast interest in crime and Wheatley was
fascinated by Knight, who was the first M.I.5 man he had come
across. He realized that if he could persuade him to talk, then
vital original material would be his, either for a non-fiction
project or simply as a base for the plot of one of his thrillers.

In 1933 the Paternoster Club, composed of writers, pub-
lishers and journalists, had been formed, and by 1935 Wheatley
was chairman. The club had a distinguished membership,
including J. M. Barrie and Leslie Charteris, but it also had some
writers who were involved in secret activities, such as Knight,
George Hill (who was later to go into the Special Operations
Executive and whose registration card openly stated that he had
been in the 'secret service'), and, of course, Tom Driberg.

[1] *Drink and Ink: Memoirs, 1919–1977* (Hutchinson, 1979).

Knight found the Paternoster Club, which met regularly on the first Wednesday of each month for lunch, an excellent source of information and a potential recruiting ground. His registration card for 1935 read:

N ....Knight, Maxwell, F., R.G.S., F.Z.S., F.R.M.S.
PRO.OCC.BUS   Author.
P.ADD   38, Sloane Street, SW1 P .... Sloane 3093
M.OR S...............Widower
PUBLISHER ....(G.B.) Philip Allan
S.SUB.................Criminology, Boxing, Cricket, also 18th Century period.
REC....................Fishing, Cricket, Fencing, Photography.
O.OF C ....Educated for the Navy, H.M.S. Worcester 1915–1917. Served in Navy during the war, 1917–1919. Ministry of Shipping, 1919–1920. Schoolmaster, 1920–1924. Freelance work 1925–1927. Manager of Sporting Hotel, 1927–1930. F.R.M.S. First novel published September, 1934, "Crime Cargo". (Philip Allan). "Gunman's Holiday" May, 1935.
CLUBS ....Overseas, Authors, Surrey County Cricket Club

In 1936, the year after the trauma of Gwladys's death, Knight went to a hunting, shooting, and fishing pub in Aldermaston – in atmosphere rather similar to the Royal Oak – where he met Lois Coplestone. Lois was ten years younger than Knight, a county lady who lacked Gwladys's spirit but was competititve and strong willed.

'Max was a deeply charming person,' Lois remembers, 'and I was immediately attracted to him in Aldermaston. We spent a lot of time in the country together and he taught me to fish.'

Because he was older, Lois was a little in awe of him, and with her he played his by now somewhat familiar avuncular role. She was fascinated by his cloak and dagger life, although Knight confided in her rather prosaically that his current amibition was to be a prison governor. She met his 'fat, jolly sister Enid' and grew very fond of her.

Knight married Lois in 1937, installing her in his flat in Sloane Street among a menagerie of animals which now included a white bull-terrier, a piping bullfinch, a bush-baby and a blue-fronted Amazon parrot who unfortunately took a personal dislike to her. Nevertheless, Lois was soon aware of the bond of understanding and trust that existed between Knight and his creatures, a bond that she could never share.

Knight confided in Lois about Gwladys, although he did not mention the sexual problems. He simply said that they had drifted apart and that he blamed himself for her loneliness. Lois realized how shattered he had been by what had happened. Knight had yet to consummate their own marriage. Like Gwladys, Lois decided to be patient and to live in hope.

'We didn't lead much of a social life and often we used to sit in the dark in Sloane Street because it was the animals' bedtime! A few people came to dinner – I remember Vernon Kell, the Wheatleys and Dennis Wheatley's stepson, Bill Younger, who began working for Max. One thing I gradually discovered about Max as we lived together at Sloane Street was that he liked to control people.'

Because of the successful conclusion of the Woolwich Arsenal case, Kell and Liddell were strong in their praise of Knight and his standing in M.I.5 was restored. Kell had now realized that counter-subversion should be centralized in one specific unit and he appointed Knight to bring this about. The new department would need to contain a group of highly sophisticated, well informed young men and women and Knight was asked to begin recruiting. He also continued his policy of regarding the strongest arm of counter-subversion as long-term counter-intelligence. Olga Gray's infiltration had been positive evidence of this. Her greatest value lay in the fact that she was there before the event itself, i.e. she was an accepted part of the organization well before Glading approached her.

So far, M.I.5 had largely been concerned with Soviet espionage, but with the rise to power of the Nazis, German espionage was a real threat. As a result it was decided that the right wing must come under surveillance and the initiative for infiltration was left to Knight's counter-subversion department.

On 9 February 1933, the Oxford Union had passed the celebrated motion that 'this House will not fight for King and Country'; shortly after this, Bill Younger, then up at Oxford, had been recruited by Knight to spy on his university friends. Knight was anxious to learn how many of the undergraduates were really dangerous agitators, secretly paid by Moscow or the Nazis, as opposed to the many hundreds of idealistic youngsters.

Wheatley wrote later that 'Max Knight whom we afterwards always referred to as "uncle", asked if we would object to Bill's being asked if he would undertake a secret investigation. Naturally, we agreed and so did Bill.'[2] Bill Younger's 'secret investigation' meant reporting back on possible subversives directly to Knight or his tutor at Christ Church, J. C. Masterman, who was also working for M.I.5. Masterman had been imprisoned during World War I at Ruhleben in Germany, a camp which had some of the worst conditions on record. His experiences there turned him into a patriot whose sympathies were entirely against the Oxford Union resolution. The press had been largely condemnatory, with the *Express* asserting that Oxford students were 'woozy-minded Communists and sexual indeterminates', the *Telegraph* accusing them of 'foul-minded disloyalty', while *The Times* contented itself with a leading article headed 'Children's Hour', in which the students were said to epitomize Britain's decadence by simply being too young to know any better. The St. John's College Boat Club marched on the Union and tried to tear the resolution out of the minute

[2] *Drink and Ink.*

book, Churchill thundered on about his nausea at the 'abject, squalid, shameless avowal' made in the Oxford Union and 275 white feathers were sent to the Union President, Frank Hardie.

It was against this background that Younger began his investigations. He soon found that the union was dominated by the left wing and it was possible to be president of the Labour Club and still call yourself a Communist. One of the popular songs of the time was:

Redshirts, blackshirts, everybody come!
Join the Oxford Labour Club and make yourselves at home.
Bring your Marx and Engels and squat upon the floor
And we'll teach you economics as you never heard before.

The Communist association itself, the October Club, flourished, although its meetings were often broken up by rugger-playing hearties and occasionally banned by the proctors. The young Communists who were only playing at belief dubbed each other 'Comrade', sang 'The Red Flag' and often went on to the Carlton Club for drinks.

Younger was later to be recruited to Knight's counter-subversion department and he also worked for some years after the war in a variety of M.I.5 roles. Stricken by polio as a boy, he was left with the legacy of a withered arm, poor health and stunted growth. An imaginative poet, he had nevertheless wanted to join the Foreign Office but, having failed to get a First at Oxford because of renewed illness, he jumped at the opportunity of joining M.I.5. Younger had a deep hatred of both Communism and Fascism. He was so secretive about his activities in M.I.5 that the Wheatleys nicknamed him 'the bearded oyster'. But Younger was courageous and he attended many Communist meetings, carrying knuckledusters in his pocket in case of trouble.

This knuckledusting poet was a remarkably versatile agent and became as close to Knight as anyone could. The two men shared a sympathetic understanding, and although Knight was no intellectual he enjoyed the classical structure of Younger's poetry.

In 1935, Hutchinson published a collection of Younger's poems called *Madonna and Other Poems*, of which Howard Spring was to make the grandiose claim that 'William Younger is writing better poetry than Byron did at his age.' Younger went on to published two more collections, one of which, *The Dreaming Falcons*,[3] he dedicated to 'CHMK in gratitude'.

Knight and Bill Younger were both interested in reincarnation, inspired by a friend of the Wheatleys, Joan Grant, who dictated her books while in a trance. Dutifully taken down from his reposing wife by Leslie, her barrister husband, *The Winged Pharaoh*, published in 1937, was the first. She later left Leslie for Charles Beatty, who was a student of the occult as well as a researcher into ancient religions. Once again in a trance, Joan dictated the next two books, *Life as Carola* and *Return to Elysium*, to Charles. But Knight and Wheatley believed that Charles was so concerned with occult ceremonies and symbols that his influence caused 'a decline in her direct communication with the Powers of Light'.

Younger, heavily influenced by the ideas of Joan and Charles Grant, wrote a poem entitled 'Vision' in his collection dedicated to Max, based on a line from Joan Grant's *Life as Carola*, 'I have seen the wisdom of the gods as fire.' After the war, Younger no longer wrote poems, concentrating on producing detective stories under the satisfying pseudonym of William Mole.

While keeping young Communists under surveillance at Oxford, Knight was observing with growing concern the activities of the extreme Right. Once again playing a waiting game, he was noting the growth of violence between extremists on both sides and asssessing how these might link up with foreign ideologies such as Hitler's Nazi Germany and Mussolini's Fascist Italy.

Oswald Mosley and the British Union of Fascists, founded in 1932, had come under the particularly careful scrutiny of

[3] (Hutchinson, 1944).

Knight's department. Mosley had started his political career as a Labour M.P. His proposals for the solution of Britain's economic problems were rejected and ignored, and he resigned from the Labour Cabinet in May 1930, on the grounds that too little was being done for the unemployed and that he wanted to 'strengthen his position in the party'. Then in the late autumn of the same year, facing failure at the Labour Party conference, he took advantage of backing from Lord Nuffield and decided to launch the New Party of 'Young Nationalists'. In February 1931, Mosley officially left the Labour Party, launching the New Party on 1 March. By May, however, Mosley found that rather than gaining the backing of young people of the Left, he was receiving more and more support from those of the Right, who were themselves leaning strongly towards Fascism. As a result, some former members of the Labour Party who had defected with Mosley – including John Strachey – left to join the C.P.G.B.

The New Party's performance at the October election was disastrous, with twenty-two of the twenty-four candidates losing their deposits. All were ignominiously defeated. Mosley therefore decided to reassess the situation completely and, after keeping out of the public eye, visiting Mussolini's Italy and going through a period of indecision, he launched the British Union of Fascists on 1 October 1932. Mosley later stated that the B.U.F. was formed 'to advocate a practical policy capable of being put into immediate operation in order to meet a specific plan for the crisis in Britain', and certainly the crisis Mosley was concerned with was very real. There were almost three million unemployed in 1932, the fleet had recently mutinied at Invergordon and the economic situation was highly unstable. What Mosley promised to the beleaguered population of Great Britain was a strong, well-organized order. Their enemies, he claimed, were the enemies of the country – the Communists. At that time there was no mention of the Jews.

Regrettably, B.U.F. meetings were tinged with violence almost from the very beginning. By December 1932 Mosley was already complaining that an organized band of Communists were setting out to destroy his public occasions. As a result, he created the Fascist Defence Force, who used considerable violence in dealing with hecklers and other disruptors.

In order to monitor Mosley's personnel and future plans Knight had already planted a number of infiltrators in the B.U.F., although none of these was on M.I.5's permanent pay-roll. It soon became clear, however, that the distinctive and highly unfortunate Blackshirt uniform, with all its overtones of a paramilitary force, was providing considerable provocation. In addition, Mosley's open admiration for Hitler was unleashing anti-Semitism and he was deeply hated by the Jewish communities. Mosley had in fact given strict instructions that no B.U.F. speeches or material should contain anything anti-Semitic and had stated, as early as January 1933, that 'we do not attack Jews because they are Jews, we only attack them if we find them pursuing an anti-British policy, any Jew who is not anti-British will always get a square deal with us.' Nevertheless, Mosley was still looked on by both the public and the press as being anti-Semitic and he certainly attracted anti-Semites such as William Joyce (later Lord Haw-Haw and already under Knight's surveillance), and also gave intellectual and social respectability to groups such as the very definitely anti-Semitic Right Club. This was led by Captain Archibald Maule Ramsay, who was later interned with Mosley, and who was to form the centre-piece of Knight's next big case.

With the hardening of Mosley's attitude towards the Jews, Knight was now surrounded by Jewish informers, all anxious to implicate Mosley in as many treasonable activities as possible. But Knight knew he still had to bide his time.

Much the same applied to the Communist Party: it was all a waiting game. There were, however, certain situations where agents could operate on a shorter-term basis and, still riding high on Olga Gray's success, Knight grew more confident as Kell put greater trust in him. He began to deploy agents in many different areas and used his social contacts and his friends to help him. He even unbent to the extent of employing people from other compartments of his life. For instance, Robert

Blockey, a professional ornithologist and assistant curator of that Haslemere Educational Museum, was sent on two bird-watching expeditions to Heligoland between 1936 and 1938; the object was to report back on the fortifications the Germans were building there. David Lloyd paints an interesting picture of Knight at this time, underlining the fact that he was now dressing the part of the spy-master:

'My wife often says how sinister he looked with his tall figure and aquiline features (he himself always said he had a nose like a Jewish bookmaker), wearing a mackintosh and a brown trilby with a turned-down brim.'

When Lloyd moved to London in 1937 he took a two-roomed flat in Dolphin Square, which Knight borrowed on several occasions for meeting agents, emphasizing that Lloyd was to tell the landlord that he had allowed 'Mr. King'[4] to occupy it.

Then Knight's sister-in-law Rosamund married an Italian, Gino Sezzi, who fell foul of Mussolini and was imprisoned in the islands for some time, before being allowed to return to the mainland. Knight plotted his escape to England, and hearing that Lloyd was embarking on a motoring holiday to Switzerland and Italy, he asked him to reconnoitre various frontier posts to check how tight the security was. Eventually, however, Sezzi escaped by boarding a ship in Genoa under the pretence of seeing off a friend, and hiding in the lavatory until they were out to sea.

Once Sezzi was in England, Knight asked him to infiltrate the Italian community in Soho with the aim of discovering any subversives, and while they looked for a flat the Sezzis lived with the Knights in Sloane Street. Rosamund Sezzi felt that the Knights' marriage was going badly wrong. She remembers meeting him in the kitchen late at night. Both of them suffered from insomnia and Knight would unburden himself to her.

'First of all he told me all about the tragic death of Gwladys and how badly he felt about her. He said he hadn't been able to make a go of it.'

[4] This was one of Knight's many cover names.

Knight told Rosamund that he was seeing a doctor about his problem and went on to talk about his sense of failure. She felt desperately sorry for him.

'Max didn't seem very social and they certainly didn't entertain very much. He used to play a lot of jazz records and through him I developed a very strong love of the whole movement. He always gave the impression of being much older than Lois. He also had quite a few young henchmen, I suppose from M.I.5, and they would sometimes come to dinner.'

Lois herself was very concerned about the 'young henchmen'. Looking back on those days she reflected sadly that Knight seemed to be drifting away from her in the few years before the war and she became more and more convinced that he was being unfaithful.

'At first I thought it must be another woman, but then these male hangers-on kept appearing and their numbers increased.'

Initially, Lois thought they were merely office colleagues talking shop but, after a while, she became convinced that they meant a good deal to him. She remembered being very angry when one young man calmly walked into the room when she was dressing.

'That was the first time I was really furious with Max. Our marriage still hadn't been consummated and I was desperately hurt and lonely. Naturally, I thought I was unattractive – that there was something repulsive about me. If only Max could have been honest with me,' claimed Lois in hindsight, 'and brought himself to tell me that he was increasingly attracted to men, then we could have faced the problem together for I loved him and I had been sure he loved me.'

In 1937, on a long lonely walk with her dog, Lois met Joanna St. Johnston and invited her and her husband back to the flat. Eric St. Johnston, later to become Commissioner of New Scotland Yard, was then doing a year's practical training as a police constable at Vine Street police station in the West End. He and his wife were both immediately attracted to Knight's strong personality. Knight told Eric St. Johnston that he was a civil servant at the War Office, but the St. Johnstons were to realize that Knight was a civil servant with a difference when he introduced them to some of his pets – salamanders, assorted snakes and a bush-baby.

It was only later that Eric St. Johnston, quite by chance, discovered the real nature of Knight's work. Patrolling in Half Moon Street, he happened to notice that a hotel called Flemings seemed to back directly on to another hotel in Clarges Street. Walking round the back to Clarges Street, St. Johnston discovered that there was another hotel with a completely different name exactly opposite Flemings. That evening, wearing plain clothes, he went into Flemings, had a drink at the bar, walked through the building, had another drink at the bar of the other hotel and went out into the next street. He realized that this Alice-in-Wonderland set-up could easily pose problems for the police, particularly as to the question of where one licensee's responsibilities ended and the other's began. He therefore submitted a report to his superiors, but heard nothing more of it. A few months later Knight told St. Johnston that he had just read the interesting report he had made about the two hotels.

'This surprised me greatly because I had no idea that he, in the course of his work, was interested in that sort of thing. He then disclosed to me that he was in fact a member of M.I.5, and that this hotel had been a place of interest to his office because it was a meeting place for people who were believed to be in sympathy with the Nazi party.'

Dennis and Joan Wheatley were also constant visitors to the flat, but Lois found she had little in common with Knight's and Wheatley's – and to some extent Joan Wheatley's – all-absorbing interest in the occult and, in particular, Aleister Crowley, who was later to become an M.I.5 agent. Wheatley had met Crowley through Tom Driberg, then a remarkable journalist (and later a Labour M.P.) whom Knight was to use as an agent inside the C.P.G.B. Crowley had come to dinner with the Wheatleys several times and had provided Dennis with occult information for his books. Wheatley's first opinion had been that Crowley was interesting but harmless. Driberg, however, warned him that Crowley had been responsible for running a community in northern Sicily where a number of children had been rumoured to have disappeared in connection with satanic masses. He also told Wheatley that there had been another alarming episode, this time in Paris, which was better documented. In an attempt to raise the pagan god, Pan, Crowley had spent the night in an empty hotel room on the Left Bank, in company with one of his followers, a man named MacAleister. In the morning they were both found naked. MacAleister was dead and Crowley was crouched howling in a corner, from where he was taken to an asylum. Four months later he was released, but the cause of MacAleister's death was never discovered. This, anyway, was Driberg's story and it fascinated both Wheatley and Knight, although Crowley in the flesh remained a disappointment.

Knight met Crowley at the Wheatleys. He was well-dressed and middle-aged, with the voice and manner of an Oxbridge don. He said his own grace, embroidering Rabelais' *Fay ce que vouldras* (Do what you like) – do what thou will shall be the whole of the law – but nevertheless Knight wondered how such racy legends had sprung up around such a seemingly harmless, if eccentric, academic.

Knight told his nephew, Harry Smith, that he and Dennis Wheatley went to Crowley's occult ceremonies to research black magic for Wheatley's books. 'They jointly applied to Crowley as novices and he accepted them as pupils,' Smith told me. 'But my uncle stressed that his interest – and also Wheatley's – was purely academic.'

As tension increased in Europe, Kell began to appreciate how much larger M.I.5 would have to become to counteract the threat from both Communists and Fascists. In 1937, therefore, he decided that Knight should move his office from M.I.5's headquarters, now at Thames House on Millbank, to Dolphin Square, a luxurious block of flats built by Richard Costain on the Thames embankment. There were two reasons for this move. Firstly, it gave Knight more secrecy for an operational department if the office was in a separate building. Secondly, Dolphin Square was within easy reach of the highly suspect Anglo-German Information Service in Parliament Street, run by Dr. R. G. Rosel, ostensibly the London correspondent of the *National-Zeitung* but in reality a Nazi propagandist. Before he was deported in May 1939, Rosel was taking a strong interest in Mosley's British Union of Fascists as well as The Link, the Anglo-German Fellowship and the more recently founded Right Club. As a result, Knight determined to increase his infiltration of the B.U.F., as well as beginning immediate investigations into the other Right-wing groups. The Anglo-German Fellowship was founded in September 1936 by Ernest Tennant, a merchant banker who had travelled widely in Germany and who was a personal friend of Ribbentrop.

'Hitler was only just in time,' he told Ashridge Conservative College in 1933. 'You cannot crush armed Communism with gloved hands. . . . When accusing the Nazis of wanton brutality it must be remembered that the alternative – a Communist revolution – might have been worse.'

The only alternatives to Hitler that Tennant could see were 'Allied reoccupation of Germany by armed force' or 'civil war and chaos followed by Bolshevism'. He condemned the way the Jews were being treated but recommended that 'our press should pay more attention to the conservative side of the Hitler movement.' Aimed at the rich and influential, the Anglo-German Fellowship sought, as one of its annual reports stated, 'to promote fellowship between the two peoples'. But in essence the organization was a society of businessmen who, although not necessarily approving of Nazi policy, were anxious to improve commercial links. At the same time, however, there is no doubt that the more extreme members used this moderate platform as a means of presenting Nazi Germany in a more respectable light. Members included F. C. Tiarks (Governor of the Bank of England), Lord Redesdale, the Duke of Wellington, Lieutenant-Colonel Sir Thomas Moore, Lord Londonderry, Prince and Princess von Bismarck, Dr. Fritz Hesse, Admiral Sir Murray Sueter and Admiral Sir Barry Domvile, among many other distinguished military, business, banking and aristocratic people.

The Link was founded in 1937 as an 'independent non-party organization to promote Anglo-German friendship' and by 1939 it had thirty-five branches. The majority of these, however, were not extremist and devoted themselves to German wine and food evenings, garden parties, debates and other similar activities. With a membership of well over 4,000 by just before the war, including a strong naval following, its main publication was the *Anglo-German Review*. This, however, was a propaganda platform for Goebbels and the organization was run by Admiral Sir Barry Domvile, who held very pro-Nazi views as well as being highly anti-Semitic. As a result The Link became more and more political and the central London branch, founded in 1939, was determinedly anti-Semitic and pro-Nazi. One of the speeches, 'Secret Forces Working for War', was delivered by Captain Ramsay. Knight was particularly interested in Ramsay, whose Right Club was soon to come under the increased scrutiny of M.I.5.

In March 1939 the Secretary of State for Home Affairs, trying to answer a question in the House about The Link from Geoffrey Mander, M.P., said:

'I understand that this organization is mainly for the purposes of pro-Nazi and anti-Semitic propaganda.'

Domvile responded by stating that 'The Link's sole object is to promote better relations between the British and German peoples by non-political means.' But although Domvile had written in September 1938 that 'the Jews of Germany have been harshly treated, and the undoubted persecution that has taken place is strongly deprecated' he nevertheless added: 'This persecution has been grossly exaggerated in our newspapers, whilst the very real grievances of the German people against the Jews have never been placed before the British public.'

In the manner of the period, Knight often made anti-Semitic jokes, but his real feelings about Jewish communities stemmed from common English prejudice and a fear of the unknown. He took, as always, a Buchan line, although the attitude Buchan expressed in most of his fiction was a far cry from his real interest in Zionism, which started in 1930. One of his biographers, Janet Adam Smith, writes: 'If "Jew" had once – though with many personal exceptions – suggested to Buchan either a seedy adventurer on the Rand or a plushy financier in Park Lane, now it suggested a man of vision and enterprise, a pioneer, a practical idealist.' Indeed, in his novel *The Four Hostages* Buchan made one of his heroes a Jew. The problem with Knight's thinking was that it had not progressed as far as Buchan's and, like the majority of the population who secretly applauded Mosley's own unintentional anti-Semitism, he was heavy-handed in his Englishman's view of Jewry.

The friendship between Knight and Wheatley continued to flourish. Gradually, Knight's world of intrigue began to encroach into Wheatley's life, a process that was received more than willingly. Yet the way this was done, in open correspondence, paints an extraordinary picture of the amateurishness of M.I.5's pre-war operations. One letter, for instance, openly discusses the surveillance of Dartington Hall, the progressive school and music centre in Devon run by Leonard Elmhirst and Dorothy Whitney, whose son, Michael Straight, was recruited as an undergraduate by Blunt to spy for what is now the K.G.B. The environment of Dartington was radical and was considered by Knight to be a breeding-ground for Communism.

Two months later, early in 1939, Knight asked Wheatley to employ an Austrian refugee, Frau Friedl Gaertner,[5] who was to pose as a part-time research assistant to the Wheatleys but in fact was to report back to Knight on the current activities of various German nationals in Britain. Friedl had a sister respectably married to Ian Menzies, younger brother of Major-General Sir Stewart Menzies (Head of M.I.6), but Friedl was in fact a double agent, the Abwehr having recruited her in 1938 before she came to England. Knight was fully aware of this from other sources.

[5] Her M.I.5 code name was Gelatine.

71

On 5 January 1939, Knight wrote to Wheatley about Frau Gaertner, and although he writes obliquely his natural sense of intrigue and melodrama comes through.

> 38 Sloane Street
> SW1
>
> 5 January, 1939
>
> Dear Dennis,
>
> Very many thanks for your most interesting letter of the 4th, which in itself might be quite useful, and if any further items of general news occur to you I shall be most grateful if you would let me have them.
>
> I am still very uncertain about the 11th, I am afraid, but at least you understand how I am placed.
>
> With regard to the particular business which we have been discussing. I should very much like to bring my friend along to see you early next week, but I rather feel we ought to have another talk before then, as it is absolutely essential for the scheme and for her own peace of mind that she should not suspect that the job is not an entirely genuine one. I will ring you up if I may in the next day or so and see what we can fix.
>
> Best wishes from us both for 1939.
>
> Yours ever,
>
> Max

By 11 January Frau Gaertner had met the Wheatleys and been approved. It is interesting to note, however, that despite their friendship and the almost reckless frankness of their correspondence, Knight never told the Wheatleys that Frau Gaertner was a double agent.

> 38 Sloane Street
> London, S.W.1
>
> My dear Dennis,
>
> I just want to write a line to thank you very much indeed for all the trouble you have taken in the particular

matter we were discussing last night, and for the extremely able way in which you have co-operated. I must say, after last night's interview I came to the conclusion that when you turned your attention to literature the intelligence department lost a great opportunity, though I fear the financial rewards in literature are greater than in the world of intrigue!

I do hope that the enterprise will actually be successful from your point of view. My only fear is that we may find some difficulty in getting hold of the references which are required. However, I have no doubt there is some way of getting round that.

In the meanwhile you have certainly earned my sincere gratitude, and in our friend you have acquired another Dennis Wheatley fan!

All the very best,

Yours ever,

Max

The fact that Max was writing to Wheatley openly about providing a cover job for an agent was amazing enough, but the additional fact that he also makes a reference to the intelligence department itself is staggering. It was this kind of carelessness that allowed such easy Soviet penetration of M.I.5 during the Second World War.

The correspondence continued, with Knight making arrangements for Frau Gaertner to receive a limited work permit while at the same time tapping Wheatley for more information. Once again, however, despite the scrawled 'Personal' on top of the letter, Knight was running a tremendous risk by openly writing about such matters. It seems strange that he did not speak to Wheatley personally. Knight's self-dramatization may have had something to do with it, for he continuously tried to ensure Wheatley realized that the real-life security services were equally, if not more, interesting than anything Wheatley could create in his books.

By March 1939 Frau Gaertner had settled into the Wheatley

household and Knight was arranging payment. He was also taking a personal interest in offering a permanent job to Bill Younger. Knowing that Kell would appreciate Younger's intuitive abilities and good social connections on a permanent basis, Knight wrote in a letter to Wheatley of 21 July 1939:

There is a possibility of a vacancy in our own office, probably of a temporary nature, salary about £300 a year. This job would be for what one might term 'the duration of the crisis and/or war'. It would be temporary in the sense that if suddenly there was a wonderful peace move and things really looked like settling down, it would of course be necessary for us to cut down staff and therefore the last to come would have to be the first to go. I think that the work would be exceedingly good training for the other job, and I have been given to understand that acceptance of a temporary job with us would not prevent Bill's name from going back on the rota for the other job later.

What do you think of this idea? The advantage is that Bill would feel that he was doing something useful and gaining experience, and of course it is impossible to say exactly when vacancies may occur in the other quarter. If you like to let me know by return what your personal view is – that is to say that you and Joan have no objection – I will push on the matter and put Bill's name forward.

With regard to our mutual lady friend: may I take it that if I send the usual cash to your house it will be opened and dealt with by your secretary, or shall I settle up direct with our friend, saying that you have asked me to do this?

I hope you are having a good rest and enjoying better weather than we are here, where it is beyond any description.

Yours ever,
Max

In September Knight asked for Wheatley's assistance in sounding out another potential agent, and Wheatley did his best to help.

Dear Dennis,

Re Ahmed: Very many thanks for your notes. I should be grateful if you would sound him out very gently particularly with a view to finding out if he would be willing to do this sort of work abroad. When I hear from you I can then take some further steps.

Yours ever,

M.

By this stage Wheatley was anxious to lend himself to the war effort, at first with the Ministry of Information, and Knight tried to pull as many strings as he was able. But Wheatley found difficulties in getting into the Ministry of Information and, nursing a secret ambition to join M.I.5, he continued to give Knight every assistance he could.

As the shadows of war lengthened, Knight realized that the biggest test of his department was about to come. On the strength of the successful conclusion to the Woolwich Arsenal case, Knight's new department in Dolphin Square had complete autonomy and was quite separate from the rest of M.I.5. In the next five years, this autonomy was to be one of Knight's most vital assets.

CHAPTER SIX

WAR: JOAN MILLER AND THE TYLER KENT CASE: 1939–1940

JOAN MILLER,[1] recruited by Knight just before war was declared, was to become one of his most talented associates. Knight (now given the military rank of Captain) was not only able to make strong relationships with women but he also had a rare ability to equip them as successful agents. Like Olga Gray, Joan Miller was an upper-class girl of great spirit. Her background was extremely unstable. Her parents, whose lives consisted mostly of parties and pleasure, consigned their child to the care of a succession of nannies and then sent her to boarding school. This in itself was not unusual for upper-class children of the time, but even in the holidays Joan was rarely at home with her parents. She spent most of them with relatives, growing up lonely and rootless. Eventually her father gambled away the family fortune and then deserted the family, divorcing her mother and marrying again. Unable to cope, her mother took to drink and later died of alcoholism.

[1] Joan Miller (or Joanna Phipps as she was later known) died suddenly in June 1984. In old age, like Olga Gray, she was bored and restless. She was also embittered by what she considered was Knight's bad treatment of her. Highly insecure, she had been unable to take his rejection, and many of her allegations against him have to be seen in that light. Nevertheless, she was a person of great drive and talent and I grew to like her very much as I interviewed her. She plied me with gin and smoked salmon in great quantities. Joan did nothing by halves – that was her style.

When she left school, Joan went to work as a mail clerk at Elizabeth Arden. After learning to type she worked her way into Arden's advertising department and was eventually able to afford a flat in Chelsea. In many ways, Joan Miller achieved an entrée into society just as Knight had done; they both talked their way into good connections. Knight relied on his charm and Joan on her looks.

Again like Olga Gray, Joan Miller was recruited by a woman, this time by an old school friend, Janet Withers, who worked in M.I.5's registry, a complex card-index system which listed the background and movements of organizations or individuals considered potentially or actively subversive. Janet Withers wondered if Joan would like a job as 'exciting as her own', and Joan, who was now bored with Arden's and was living the life of a débutante, had exactly the same reaction as Knight had had, years before, to the offer of a job in M.I.5. It sounded exciting, glamorous and mysterious. For someone almost alone in the world it provided not only civil service security but also the feeling of joining an exclusive club.

'I want all my girls to be well bred and have good legs,' Kell had said, and certainly Joan Miller more than qualified. She was also able to supply some excellent references. So, in September 1939, just before the outbreak of hostilities, Joan was told to arrive at a bus stop opposite the Natural History Museum in South Kensington at 9 a.m. and board an unmarked bus that would be waiting there. She found there were other girls on the bus; they drove to Wormwood Scrubs in total silence. The expanded M.I.5 had been moved into the cells of the Scrubs as the prison was erroneously thought to be bomb-proof. On her first day all was chaos, with prisoners still being evacuated as M.I.5 staff moved in.

Replacing a secretary who was no longer able to cope with the pressure, Joan worked for Lord Cottenham, who was in charge of M.I.5's transport pool. For some months she continued in this routine job, quietly enjoying contact with the famous names and distinguished faces around her. Security was lax; among the staff were men like Blunt, an ex-Communist and homosexual;

and apparently the bus conductors used to call out 'Anyone for M.I.5?' as their buses stopped outside.

One of the more perceptive employees of M.I.5, commenting on the Scrubs at the time, said it was full of hunting and fishing types when what were actually required were typists and filing clerks. The farcical element increased as Kell's fashionable young women, unable to treat working for M.I.5 seriously, brought hampers and shooting-sticks so that they could picnic in the fields around the prison.

Knight, realizing how chaotic security was at the Scrubs, kept his distance at Dolphin Square, although occasionally he came over to the canteen to eat. But Joan had heard rumours about his department, which was now known as B5(b) to mark its exclusive concern with infiltrating agents into potentially sub-versive groups, mainly either Communist or Fascist, within Britain.

It was in fact Bill Younger who first told Joan that Knight had been watching her for some time. Strikingly good-looking, Joan was ambitious, extrovert and extremely sophisticated. Although she was more sociable than Olga Gray and much more domineering, she had the same drive and spirit that Knight recognized as good qualities in his women agents. Again, she was also someone who was very much on her own. Younger suggested that she might like to work for Knight and Joan lunched with Knight in the canteen. Like Olga, she found his charm fascinating and his voice hypnotic. This was what she had been hoping for – a man who looked and behaved like a suave spy-master, not just an aristocratic bureaucrat. Knight told her that he wanted her to do a job for him but she would need to work in the Dolphin Square flat first. Elated, she agreed, at the same time realizing shrewdly that she would have agreed to practically anything he suggested.

Knight himself had now moved into 308 Hood House, a flat in Dolphin Square belonging to Lois's brother, and he had established B5(b) there, displaying Lois's maiden name, Miss Coplestone, above the door-bell. (Lois at this time was living mainly in the country.) This was where he interviewed agents and had his most private discussions. Joan, however, was to work in 10 Collingwood House, another flat in the square which was owned by M.I.5. There she found she was to function as Knight's personal secretary until such time as she was ready for the 'job'.

On arrival she discovered that Knight had gathered around him some versatile new case officers, all of whom had highly individual qualities. Apart from Younger, who was Knight's personal assistant, there was John Bingham, the distinguished journalist and thriller writer, who was Knight's deputy; Philip Brocklehurst, another ex-journalist; Norman Himsworth, who was responsible for supervising anti-Communist operations; playboy Tony Gillson; Rex Land; Guy Poston; and Joan Wheatley (Dennis's wife) who was responsible for fuelling their motor pool. All were young, rich and imaginative, hand-picked by Knight for their acumen, tenacity and loyalty.

John Bingham, later Lord Clanmorris and one of the models for John Le Carré's[2] Smiley, remembers Knight as 'a tremendous leader. He loved the intrigue of it all and we would follow him anywhere.'

M.I.5's wartime press officer, the writer Derek Tangye, describes Knight as 'an untouchable type of character', and in his autobiography[3] he quotes Knight anonymously, pinpointing his most prophetic statement:

> Soon after I joined M.I.5, one of the most experienced and imaginative amongst my colleagues said to me 'The Russians are very patient. They will recruit a young man at university with Communist views, tell him to dissociate himself from the Party, watch him, and keep him on ice for years. Then one day they will come to him and say: "Now we want you to do this."'

Joan Miller was to discover these very perceptive views of Knight's as she worked for him over the next few months; later

[2] David Cornwell (the real name of John Le Carré) worked for M.I.5 in an office near Knight's after the war.
[3] *The Way to Minack* (Michael Joseph, 1968).

she realized that his warnings were not listened to. Tangye also writes: 'If such insight of Soviet methods existed within M.I.5 it is more difficult than ever to understand how Maclean, Burgess and Philby got through the net.' But of course this is no longer so surprising, considering Anthony Blunt's influential presence in M.I.5. Tangye remembered Knight as a very charming, complicated character, and felt that it was his intuition which was the most remarkable aspect of his personality.

Joan, too, was enormously impressed by Knight's methods. She also realized that she was becoming physically attracted to him and gradually they grew closer, despite the fact that he was vague about his past and she sensed that he partitioned his life, never revealing himself totally to any one person.

In February 1940, Knight decided that he could begin to use Joan as an agent, in much the same way as he had used Olga Gray but over a shorter period. For her first assignment she was to infiltrate the Right Club. Initially Joan was to assist an already established M.I.5 contact, a Mrs. Amos,[4] to monitor Captain Archibald Ramsay's activities and to acquire a list of members. No action was to be taken until the list was as complete as possible, and then it was hoped that all the members could be arrested. But in fact Joan merged so convincingly that she was able to unearth a considerable espionage operation, whose participants were no more than pawns in a far wider conspiracy to bring down the government and to make peace with Germany. The three major pawns were Captain Ramsay, Anna Wolkoff and Tyler Kent.

Captain Archibald H. Maule Ramsay was an unworldly Christian patriot who clung to the belief that the world was threatened by a three-pronged conspiracy of Jews, Bolsheviks and Freemasons. His marriage to Ismay, the daughter of a Scottish viscount, was an unhappy one, which spurred him on to focus entirely on the Right Club, founded by him in 1939. The main objective of the club was to infiltrate the City and Whitehall and to capitalize on the considerable national anti-

---

[4] Mrs. Amos's real name was Marjorie Mackie.

pathy to the Jews and Communism. Meetings of the group were often chaired by the Duke of Wellington. Membership had reached over 300 by the beginning of the war, but as soon as war was declared the Right Club was closed in case there was any possibility of it being actively pro-Nazi. William Joyce, who was one of its founder members, had gone to Germany, from where, as the infamous Lord Haw-Haw, he attempted to undermine British morale, but Ramsay, still imagining that he was being patriotic, decided that he had to fight the internal enemy, which he considered no less formidable than the Axis Powers and in some ways more dangerous. His plan was to educate the public sufficiently to maintain the atmosphere in which the phoney war might become an honourable negotiated peace. Believing Churchill to be a warmonger, Ramsay and his associates wanted to organize a parliamentary coup that would discredit him, thus bringing down the Churchill administration and replacing it with a government that would be prepared to negotiate with Hitler.

A number of influential people were partially sympathetic to this view, but in fact Ramsay himself lived in a world bordering on fantasy. He devised a badge for club members which featured an eagle and a snake and he shrouded the whereabouts of the membership list in secrecy. Overly melodramatic, Ramsay accused the press of being 'Jew-ridden' and distributed a number of pamphlets, amongst which were anti-Semitic verses such as 'Land of Pope and Jewry'.

Anna Wolkoff, occasionally described by Ramsay as his political secretary, was born in Russia in 1902 and had arrived in Britain when her White Russian father, Admiral Nicholas Wolkoff, became Naval Attaché in London at the time of the Russian Revolution. Aristocratic and vehemently anti-Bolshevik, the family sought permanent exile in London, opening a Russian tea-room in Harrington Road just opposite South Kensington underground station. The tea-room soon became a hotbed of right-wing activity, and although this had not escaped Knight's attention and he had already infiltrated her circle, he could hardly take Anna Wolkoff very seriously. While dispensing tea and caviar (reputed to be the best in London), she circulated wild anti-war rumours, and at night, or in off-duty hours, she would boo at newsreels of Churchill and put up posters and stickers on walls stating that the war was no more than a Jewish plot. She was in fact the exact stereotype of a German agent as seen in British propaganda films of the time, such as *Walls have Ears*.

Anna was dark-haired, short and unattractive. She supplemented the family income by dressmaking for the aristocracy. In her childhood she had been friendly with Princess Marina, and through this contact one of her clients was the Duchess of Windsor. She was a talented person who resented the loss of the wealth, power and citizenship of her family. She loved her country fiercely, and she would give no quarter to those forces responsible for what she considered to be its destruction.

Tyler Gatewood Kent, who is still alive in Texas, was a far more complex character than either Ramsay or Wolkoff. A descendant of the Wild West hero Davy Crockett, he was born in China, where his father was American consul, and had been educated at Princeton, the Sorbonne, Madrid University and, back in America again, the George Washington University. In 1934 Kent joined the diplomatic service and was posted to the U.S. Embassy in Moscow, where he was employed as a cipher clerk. He was an isolationist, who believed that his country should avoid involvement with Europe. Isolationism had become a powerful movement in America; the aviation hero Charles Lindbergh was a leading advocate for keeping America out of the war. Kent was convinced that Roosevelt's policy ran completely contrary to this view and that he was intending to pledge American support for the Allies without having received a mandate from the American people to do so. Kent wanted ammunition for the isolationists, and he was determined to use his position to get it.

While in Moscow, Kent was recruited by the Russians and began to steal secret documents from the Embassy and take them home, a practice that was to be a dry run for his activities

82

in London. Presumably, however, they were of little value, for he destroyed them before he came to London in October 1939. Knight considered Kent to be motivated entirely by isolationist sympathies; this may well have been the case. He may have decided to become a Russian agent in order to work indirectly towards keeping America out of the war. Following the August 1939 Ribbentrop–Molotov Pact allying the Soviet Union to Nazi Germany and before Hitler's invasion of Russia in June 1941 the interests of the two countries were theoretically running parallel. However, after the war M.I.5 reclassified Kent as primarily a Soviet agent.

Kent made no secret of his isolationist views, nor his hatred for the Jews and, ostensibly, for the Communists, so it is surprising that he received security clearance. Since the late spring of 1940, however, Anthony Blunt, constantly in touch with his Soviet case officer,[5] had joined B division under Guy Liddell, then Director, and was responsible for the surveillance in London of pro-Nazi sympathizers. It may well have been through his influence that Kent received security clearance.

At the American Embassy in London Kent's job was again that of a cipher clerk, responsible for the decoding and coding of top secret messages entering and leaving the Embassy. As before, he began to take material home. On the BBC television programme, *Newsnight*, broadcast on 3 December 1982, Tyler Kent told Robert Harris:

> One of the ways that this was done was simply that I took copies which were surplus and were to be discarded, burnt in an incinerator. That was one source. Another source was that Ambassador Kennedy was having copies of important political documents made for his own private collection, and part of my function was to make these copies. And it was quite easy to slip in an extra carbon.

At that time, Roosevelt was campaigning to be re-elected President and, as the American people were 83 per cent opposed

[5] Code named Henry (in reality Anatoli Gorski).

to entering the war, he was publicly making speeches such as 'I hope the United States will keep out of this war. I believe it will, and I give you assurance and reassurance that every effort of your government will be directed toward that end. As long as it remains within my power to prevent, there will be no blackout of peace in the United States.'

Privately, however, Roosevelt was conducting a correspondence with Churchill to the effect that they would try to oust Chamberlain, put an end to the 'phoney war' and meet the Nazis head-on in open conflict. This highly secret correspondence, monitored and collected by Kent, continued after Churchill became Prime Minister in the spring of 1940, but in public Roosevelt hypocritically continued to bring out his tag line 'I've said it before and I'll say it again: I will not send American boys to die in any foreign war.' At last Kent had his ammunition – and what ammunition. If the correspondence with Churchill had been publicly released there is little doubt that Roosevelt would have lost the election. A Republican candidate would very likely have kept America out of the war, forcing England's surrender.

There was also a strong British interest in demolishing Churchill, who had rendered himself vulnerable by carrying out the correspondence directly with Roosevelt, writing the letters in the U.S. Embassy itself and having no recourse to his colleagues, despite the fact that he later claimed Chamberlain knew of his action. Churchill signed himself Naval Person (he was First Lord of the Admiralty) and sent the letters over Ambassador Kennedy's head; the Ambassador would often read them only when they had been transmitted. But Kent still needed the right opportunity to expose the negotiations, and early in 1940 it seemed as if he had found it.

What Kent did not know was that he had been watched by Knight since 8 October 1939 – three days after he arrived in England. This came about quite by accident. Knight was having a suspected Gestapo agent, posing as a Swedish business man named Ludwig Matthias, followed in London. Knight's tail reported back to him that Matthias had strolled into the

Cumberland Hotel at Marble Arch and visited one of the guests in his room. The guest was an American Embassy official named Tyler Kent.

Knight then made one of the risky, unorthodox decisions that were becoming his stock-in-trade and making him unpopular in other departments of M.I.5. Rather than telling Ambassador Kennedy that he had a major security risk on the staff, he decided to do nothing, but just keep Kent under surveillance and see where he might lead. Eight months later, Kent met Anna Wolkoff, who introduced him to Ramsay, and Knight had his chance to net all the conspirators together by infiltrating Joan Miller into the Right Club. Of course at this point Knight had no idea of the potentially far-reaching effects of Kent's actions, but Joan was to lead him to them.

Mrs. Amos took Joan to the Russian tea-rooms, with their polished wooden furniture and panelled walls, introducing her as a friend of her son who was serving in the Royal Naval Reserve. There Joan met Anna Wolkoff, and confided in her that she held a tedious clerical position in the War Office. Over the next few weeks she dropped in frequently, getting into conversation with the nostalgic Admiral and, with great skill, becoming friendly with the suspicious Anna. One evening she was invited to the flat above the tea-rooms with Anna and a group of friends including Mrs. Amos. Among the group she discovered Ismay Ramsay. Already Regulation 18B[6] was being used to intern foreigners with Nazi sympathies, and there was an atmosphere of some tension.

Desperately nervous, but realizing she was being vetted, Joan made it clear that she was against the war. Mrs. Amos had paved the way effectively for she was accepted by the group as a Fascist sympathizer. From then on Joan was invited to join the officially disbanded Right Club, much to Knight's delight. She received the eagle and snake badge and became involved in

---

[6] It gave the Home Secretary powers to detain 'if satisfied with respect to any particular person that with a view to preventing him acting in a manner prejudicial to the public safety or the Defence of the Realm, it is necessary to do so.'

Anna's lampooning of newsreels and fly-posting campaigns. The Right Club was expecting a German invasion at any moment and there was frequent debate, led by Anna, as to which of their opponents should be hanged from lamp-posts.

Anna then told Joan that it would be a good idea if she could get herself transferred to a government department where she could inflict major sabotage and Joan promised to do her best. She was also invited to tea by Mrs. Ramsay, and Knight saw this as an ideal way of doing some rather primitive bugging. Giving as her address Philip Brocklehurst's flat in Pond Place, Joan phoned Mrs. Ramsay, said she was expecting an important telephone call and suggested she should come to tea with her instead. Ismay Ramsay took the bait quite happily.

Knight sent a couple of Special Branch men down to do the bugging but unfortunately, having wired up the room, they found they could hear nothing on their earphones above the noise of the traffic. As a result, the windows had to be kept closed throughout the tea-party, and as it was very hot both Joan and Mrs. Ramsay suffered greatly. The Special Branch men, sitting in the bedroom cupboard with shorthand note-books, listening to the conversation on their earphones, were sweating profusely.

Disappointingly, Mrs. Ramsay gave nothing away while the two men, eventually let out of their prison when she had gone, were puce in the face from their Turkish bath hiding-place. A few days later, Mrs. Ramsay invited Joan back to tea in her own house in Onslow Square and there she too asked her to move jobs with sabotage in view. Unfortunately, this time there were no Special Branch men in the cupboard.

Now that Knight was aware that Tyler Kent had begun to associate with Anna Wolkoff, he told Joan to concentrate on watching Wolkoff carefully. Through Joan's surveillance, Knight discovered that Anna was in contact with Colonel Francesco Maringliano, who was an Assistant Naval Attaché at the Italian Embassy. This seemed to Knight to explain the fact that the German Ambassador in Rome, Hans Mackenson, was thought by the Government Code and Cipher School's intercept system to have been looking at Churchill's correspondence with Roosevelt. It now seemed likely that Anna was providing the link between Tyler Kent and the Italian Embassy.

Joan continued her friendship with Anna, who never suspected that her confidences were being abused. As Olga Gray had with Glading, Joan became fond of Anna Wolkoff, forever wondering how savagely their friendship might end.

Soon Joan discovered that Kent was showing the Churchill/ Roosevelt correspondence not only to Wolkoff but to Ramsay as well. Ramsay had decided to raise a question in the House about Churchill's apparent exclusion of Chamberlain in his contacts with Roosevelt. Curiously, he never actually got round to it, nor did he apparently voice any qualms at handling documents which had been treasonably obtained. He and Anna managed the affair very amateurishly, Wolkoff borrowing the copies at one stage, on behalf of Captain Ramsay, and taking them to a photographer who produced prints of them.

Then, out of the blue, Anna told Joan that she had been about to sent an important letter to William Joyce (by now Lord Haw-Haw) via the Italian diplomatic bag, but Colonel Maringliano had become ill. With great presence of mind Joan said she had access to the Romanian diplomatic bag and Anna, trustingly, gave Joan the letter. She of course took it straight to Knight and they went to have it decoded at Bletchley (the British code-breaking centre). Addressed to Herr W. B. Joyce, Rundfunk-haus, Berlin, it turned out to be some amateur guidelines on the kind of propaganda Joyce should be broadcasting, ending 'It is now very important that we hear more about the Jews and the Freemasons.' Knight arranged for it to be sent through and eventually it was used in one of Lord Haw-Haw's broadcasts.

An M.I.5 report reflects the importance of Joan's work: 'Tyler Kent next came to our notice at the end of February 1940 when an absolutely reliable source reported that this man was regarded as an important contact by Anna de Wolkoff of the Right Club. . . . She had described him as being pro-German in outlook and as having given her interesting diplomatic information of a confidential nature.' The report goes on to say that in mid-April 1940 Kent had given Wolkoff 'confidential information regarding the sea-battles off the coast of Norway and this information would appear to have been twisted in such a way as to make excellent anti-British propaganda.'

By mid-May 1940, the German Army had penetrated 240 miles inside Allied territory, France was about to collapse, and Britain was in a desperate situation. If America did not come to the rescue, there was little hope. Furthermore, if Ramsay chose this moment to bring the Churchill/Roosevelt correspondence to the notice of Parliament, Churchill would be discredited, which could force not only his own resignation but possibly even the fall of the Government.

On 18 May, therefore, Knight decided that it was time to act. He went to Joseph Kennedy, the American Ambassador, showed him the report on Tyler Kent, and asked him to waive diplomatic immunity and agree that Kent should be arrested. Kennedy was forced to give his permission, but not before he had made it very clear that he was absolutely furious at having been kept in the dark. M.I.5 had been shadowing Kent for seven months and the American Embassy was completely unaware that he was considered to be a security risk. Herschel V. Johnson, the American Embassy's Counsellor, remembered: 'I immediately told Captain Knight that in my opinion it was most regrettable that Scotland Yard had not informed us of these circumstances at the time. We would never have left the man in the code room if there had been the slightest ground for suspicion against him. . . . The Ambassador subsequently spoke strongly to Captain Knight on the same matter.' In fact Knight had another motive for not telling Joseph Kennedy earlier, for Kennedy, himself an isolationist and extremely anti-British, was also under the scrutiny of M.I.5.

On the morning of 20 May 1940, Knight led the raid on Kent's flat at 47 Gloucester Place, with the police, the Special Branch and a representative of the American Embassy. A Special Branch eye-witness later reported: 'A police officer turned the handle. The door was locked from the inside so he knocked. There was no answer, and he knocked again. A man's voice answered in a loud tone "Don't come in." The police officer knocked once more, and as the voice inside repeated "don't come in" Inspector Pearson crashed through the door and we all followed him in.'

Kent was standing by his bed in his pyjamas and a girl-friend was discovered in an adjoining room. Knight searched the flat while they were dressing and discovered 1,500 top secret stolen documents, neatly filed in thirty folders. It was an incredible haul which included State Department letters, messages from Box 500 (one of M.I.5's addresses) asking for F.B.I. assistance in tracking down Nazi and Fascist agents, some details of the testing of secret radio equipment and, in a folder marked 'Churchill', eight top secret messages from Churchill to Roosevelt which, if released, would definitely have ruined all chances of Roosevelt's re-election and America's entry into the war. One of the eight messages from Churchill had been written a few hours earlier and was in fact a desperate appeal for help. He talked of the situation being 'full of danger' and asked for destroyers and 'the largest possible number of Curtiss P40 fighters. . . . If members of the present Administration were finished and others came in to parley amid the ruins, you must not be blind to the fact that the sole remaining bargaining counter with Germany would be the fleet. . . . Excuse me, Mr. President, putting this nightmare bluntly.'

There is little doubt that despite his involvement with Wolkoff and Ramsay, Kent's main intention had been to smuggle the Churchill/Roosevelt correspondence to America to strengthen the isolationist cause. The documents, however, were not the only discovery Knight made in Kent's flat. He also found the membership list of the Right Club, apparently handed to Kent by Ramsay for safe keeping, and two duplicate keys to the Embassay code room.

A few hours later, Knight gave the Home Secretary, Sir John Anderson, a comprehensive report on Kent's activities, as well as those of the Right Club. In the report Knight stated, quite erroneously, that Ramsay was an associate of Mosley's, in a bid to find an excuse for at last arresting and interning Mosley, his wife Diana and his followers. Ramsay was a crude eccentric whose ideas Mosley had no time for, but in his report Knight stated that Mosley was 'in relations' with Captain Ramsay and, without any concrete evidence, poured in the right ingredients for the War Cabinet to believe that a major right-wing coup was at a far more developed and coherent stage than it could ever have been with such different, albeit right-wing, personalities and ideals involved.

Anna Wolkoff was arrested immediately and after a meeting of the War Cabinet on 22 May Ramsay was arrested the following day. Over the next few days most members of the Right Club, The Link and 800 members of the British Union of Fascists were also arrested, including Sir Oswald Mosley himself.

The first general interrogation of Kent after his arrest was held in Ambassador Kennedy's office on 20 May. The Ambassador, Knight and Mr. Herschel Johnson were among those present. Kent later stated that he did not know what to expect. He realized that he would probably not be sent back to the United States because of the sensitive nature of the documents and the fact that the American constitution would not permit a trial to take place in camera.

Knight must have found the interrogation extremely frustrating, for although Kent is usually described, somewhat dismissively, as a cipher clerk, he was in fact a highly educated man who was not easily to be browbeaten into a convenient confession.

The following edited extracts from the initial interrogation come from the American archives. The British transcript is still retained by M.I.5. I have added my own descriptive phrases in brackets.

Ambassador Kennedy began on a note of outraged paternalism, pointing out to Kent that he had involved his country in an extremely serious situation and adding: 'From the kind of family you come from – people who have fought for the United States – one would not expect you to let us all down.'

Kent replied (with irritating naivety): 'In what way?'

'You don't think you have?' (Kennedy's rage and humiliation

began to show.) 'What did you think you were doing with our codes and telegrams?'

'It was only for my own information,' said Kent (doggedly). 'Why did you have to have them?' insisted Kennedy.

Kent replied (once again with studied naivety), that he had them because he 'thought them very interesting'.

Then Knight took over the questioning and Kent tried to stall him by being as blockish as possible. Knight began by clarifying his position, pointing out that he was talking to him by invitation of his Ambassador and not 'in any way in connection with matters which concern only Great Britain at the moment'. He went on to state that he had proof that Kent had been associating with Anna Wolkoff.

Kent did not deny this and, encouraged, Knight elaborated: 'I am in a position to prove that she has a channel of communication with Germany; that she has used that channel of communication with Germany; that she is a person of hostile associations; that she is involved in pro-German propaganda, to say the least. As your Ambassador has just said, you have been found with documents in your private rooms to which he considers you have no proper title. You would be a very silly man if you did not realize that certain conclusions might be drawn from that situation, and it is for you to offer the explanation.' Knight then produced a locked, leather-bound volume and asked Kent to identify it. During the ensuing questioning Kent denied all knowledge of the volume's identity as well as the identity of the holder of the key. Eventually, however, he admitted that it had been given to him personally by Captain Ramsay, but he had not asked Ramsay what it contained.

Knight (repeating himself in frustration at Kent's attitude), then said: 'Don't you think it strange that a member of Parliament should come to you, a minor official in an Embassy, and give you a locked book to take care of for him? Now seriously, doesn't it strike you as odd that a member of Parliament should bring you a locked ledger and ask you to take care of it for him?'

But Kent, finding that his act as a political innocent was proving successful, continued to stonewall and replied that he did not know. Knight was determined to harangue him on this point and told him that he was 'adopting a sort of naive attitude that failed to deceive. You are either hiding something or . . . '

Digging in his heels, Kent insisted that Ramsay had simply handed the volume to him for safe keeping. Then Knight asked him if he knew that Captain Ramsay 'associated' with Anna Wolkoff.

'Yes, if by associated you mean he knows her,' replied Kent.

Knight showed Kent a letter to Anna Wolkoff of 21 March 1940, in which Kent had written 'I hope to see you and make the acquaintance of more of your interesting friends.'

'Who were the interesting friends?' asked Knight.

Kent replied that he was talking about Captain Ramsay and that he was interesting because 'We had a sort of common view, to a certain extent.'

Having extracted this guarded admission, Knight went straight to the heart of the matter. 'The first time that you came to my attention was in February 1940 when your friend, Anna Wolkoff, was telling people that she had made an extremely useful contact with a young man at the American Embassy. I am going to speak now extremely bluntly. I am afraid I must take the view that you are either a fool or a rogue, because you cannot possibly be in any position except that of a man who has either been made use of or who knows all these people. I propose to show you how.'

Knight then told Kent that on 16 April 1940 he received a report stating that Anna Wolkoff was giving details to some of her close associates in the Right Club of an interview between Ambassador Kennedy and Lord Halifax concerning the problems the British Navy faced over the landing of German troops in Norway. Obviously this information could only have come from Kent himself. Kent (still stonewalling) replied that he did not remember what he had said 'in conversation in April 1940'.

'You have a very good memory for what you have not said but not a very good memory for what you have said,' replied

Knight, proceeding to take the interrogation a stage further. 'Now you were in a restaurant with Matthias on October 8th, 1939. He then went and paid a short visit to your room at the Cumberland. On leaving Matthias was carrying an envelope approximately 10" × 6", which he was not carrying when he went into the hotel.'

'I certainly don't remember that incident at all,' was Kent's reply, before he went on to claim that Matthias had only come to fetch a smuggled box of cigars. In answer to subsequent questions Kent denied that he had passed on to Anna Wolkoff secret information about the North Sea war zone, telling her that the British success had been greatly exaggerated and was merely propaganda designed to cover heavy British losses sustained in the air attack on Scapa Flow. Kent further denied that he had given Anna Wolkoff secret information about radio equipment.

Knight then asked him if he had ever tried to send any communications to America via the diplomatic bag. Kent replied that, with the exception of a few letters to his immediate family, he had not. Knight shifted the questioning to William Joyce, who had just slipped through the M.I.5 net. But, once again, Kent denied all knowledge of him except that he had heard he was 'supposed to be some sort of Irishman'. Knight then turned back to the book that Ramsay had given Kent, but Kent simply repeated that he had never opened the book and knew nothing of its contents.

Returning to the documents, Knight said: 'It is not for me to discuss the question of your position with regard to these documents belonging to your Government, because that is not my affair at all. But your explanation about this appears to me to be extremely unconvincing; and your explanations of every point raised are unconvincing.'

Kent simply stuck to the unlikely answer that he had merely taken the documents for his own interest.

Finding he was up against a brick wall, Knight tried a different approach. 'You know you are in an extremely bad position. If you were English you would be in a very difficult position. You don't impress me by your cocky manner.'

'I haven't been making any attempt to be cocky or to impress you; but I say that the reason is just what I stated,' Kent replied.

Knight asked Kent if he considered Anna Wolkoff 'a loyal British subject' and Kent replied 'Well, if you mean that she holds some views that are apparently at variance with some of the ideals possibly of the British Government that is quite true; but it doesn't mean that she is not a loyal British subject.'

Knight queried whether a loyal British subject communicated secretly, and for the first time Kent appeared slightly rattled. He said, 'No, but I have absolutely no knowledge of that. This is the first I have heard of it. If you say that she is in communication with the enemy why of course she is not a loyal British subject: but when you put the question to me this morning I didn't know that.'

'But this morning you wouldn't say yes or no,' replied Knight. 'A person is either loyal or disloyal.'

'If you think that everybody that doesn't approve of what is being done by the country is disloyal that would – '

But Knight was not to be harangued and he cut in: 'Now you are merely trying to talk like a parlour politician, but we are dealing with fundamentals.'

Suddenly Kennedy intervened, pointing out to Knight that if he could prove Anna Wolkoff was in contact with the enemy then 'she is more or less a spy.' He went on to ask, 'If the United States Government decides to waive any rights they may have, do I understand that that might very well make Kent part and parcel of that?'

'Subject to the production of evidence under the law, yes. I think honestly that at this stage nothing very useful is to be got by carrying on this conversation,' Knight replied, unwilling to commit himself, particularly as he had concealed so much from Kennedy already, although he knew that it would be possible to assemble the required evidence.

To prevent any embarrassment to Roosevelt's re-election campaign, Kent and Wolkoff were held on remand throughout the summer of 1940. From Brixton, Kent kept up a battery of protest, some of which Knight sent to Herschel Johnson at the American Embassy. In one of his covering letters Knight was able to add some confidential information:

SECRET

Telephone Nos	Box No. 500
Shepherd's Bush 5391–2	Parliament Street B.O.
Acorn 3286–7	London S.W.1.

P.F. 47438/B.5B   5th June 1940

Dear Mr. Herschel Johnson,

I have been asked by the Governor of Brixton Prison to forward to you the enclosed communication from Tyler Kent, also some letters; and I'm afraid I can do nothing but comply with his request, although I am afraid you have quite enough to worry you.

Here is another piece of information which I pass on to you in confidence: Captain Ramsay has for some time past been in correspondence with one *Walter CRICK*, Hotel Collingwood, 45 West 35th Street, New York, who on April 29th, 1940, was at Cambria Pines Lodge, Cambria, California. It is clear that Walter CRICK is what one can only describe as a Fifth Columnist in the United States, and I should say a fanatic of the same type as Ramsay.

I thought it might just be worthwhile letting you know about this man, in case you care to inform your own people. It appears that he is giving Ramsay information regarding American industry and its alleged deficiencies from the point of view of exports to this country, which would be of considerable value as pro-German propaganda in England and might possibly be detrimental to the interests of your own country.

With kindest regards,
Yours sincerely,
Maxwell Knight
Capt.

On 24 February 1940 Tyler Kent had in fact written to Kirk, the Chargé d'Affaires at the American Embassy in Berlin, applying for a transfer. This implies that he would have taken the documents there, either for his own 'historical' interest, or to give to the Germans, so they could expose Roosevelt's double standards and prevent America from entering the war, or even to pass on to the Russians. The letter, which was read out in court at Kent's trial, demonstrates his guile. Having told Kirk that his transfer from Moscow to London was so abrupt that he had no time to express his own wishes, he applied for the new transfer, stating he had previously worked for Kirk when he had been Chargé d'Affaires in Moscow. His extremely articulate letter was read out at the trial which took place in camera at the Old Bailey in October 1940.

I have in mind changing places with someone on the staff there who has had enough of it in Germany and would not mind coming to London. . . . I am fully aware of all the adverse conditions of life in Germany, but I think that after my stay in Moscow I haven't much to learn about things of that sort. I am very much interested in Central and Eastern Europe and feel that I would be much happier studying conditions in Germany than remaining here in London where I have no particular interests. May I also humbly suggest that my background of knowledge of Soviet conditions and of the Russian language may at some future date prove of use to the Embassy inasmuch as Germany and Soviet Russia, to all appearances, will eventually league together against the Allies. . . . I am quite expert in the use of codes and am quite willing to continue at that work in the event I were transferred to Berlin.

Ambassador Kennedy was most annoyed to find that Tyler Kent had written this letter without consulting the American Embassy in London first, but in fact Kirk turned down Kent's suggestion, pointing out that the man he wished to exchange with no longer wanted to come to London.

For some time those on the political Left in Britain had felt very dissatisfied with Sir John Anderson, the wartime Home Secretary, considering that he was far too liberal in his approach to right-wing groups such as the B.U.F., the Right Club, The Link and, of course, the Anglo-German Fellowship. Many of the Left felt these organizations should be controlled immediately, even if British citizens were involved. Here they found an ally in Kell's deputy, Brigadier A. W. A. Harker, who did not take such a tolerant view of fifth-column activities as Anderson or Kell and who believed that Britain must be a united stronghold. Knowing that this stronghold still contained 'large numbers of persons of doubtful loyalty', he felt that 'it is clearly essential that every person within the fortress must be either harnessed to the national effort or put under proper control.'[7]

Anderson, however, felt that this was neither fair nor in the long run very wise. He considered that Mosley in particular was a patriot who would never betray his country personally, and despite the doubtful company that had been attracted to his cause Anderson was still not prepared to accept that he and his followers should be arrested. Accordingly, he submitted papers to the War Cabinet on 18 May 1940, which stated:

Although the policy of the British Union of Fascists is to oppose the war and to condemn the Government, there is no evidence that they would be likely to assist the enemy. Their public propaganda strikes a patriotic note. . . . In my view it would be a mistake to strike at this organization at this stage by interning the leaders. Apart from the fact that there is no evidence on which such action would be justified, it is to be borne in mind that premature action would leave the organization itself in being and other leaders could be appointed to take the place of those who had been apprehended. In my view we should hold our hand.

[7] British Public Record Office FO 371 25248, folio 417.

The original Emergency Powers (Defence) Bill had been introduced into the Commons by Sir Samuel Hoare on 24 August 1939, but the exact wording was not revealed as the Government was seeking the widest possible powers, although a few words were added: 'We do not intend to introduce regulations that would affect the liberty of the subject . . . until the country is actually involved in hostilities.'

On 1 September 1939 (when Germany invaded Poland) the Government issued Defence Regulations via an Order in Council which meant they did not have to go through or be debated by Parliament. The wording had been slightly modified and the clause known as 18B gave the Home Secretary powers to detain 'if satisfied with respect to any particular person that with a view to preventing him acting in a manner prejudicial to the public safety or the Defence of the Realm, it is necessary to do so.'

This regulation was favoured by the police as it gave them very wide powers, but there were so many protests in Parliament that the Home Office made considerable modifications to 18B, stating that they would detain only those of 'hostile origin or associations' or those involved in 'acts prejudicial to the public safety or the Defence of the Realm'. But the subtle point was that before the changes they could have detained people before they committed a dangerous act. Now they could take action only if the suspects were irrefutably behaving in a dangerous manner.

Sir John Anderson stated at the meeting of the War Cabinet on 18 May 1940 that it was difficult to take action when there was no evidence that an organization was involved in disloyal activities. In the timing of their raid on Tyler Kent's flat on 20 May – two days after Anderson's statement – M.I.5 took up the challenge and set out to provide evidence of the treasonable activities of the British Right. As a result of the discoveries at Tyler Kent's flat and the involvement of Anna Wolkoff, Churchill and Chamberlain received messages from M.I.5 stating the case against the entire Right, by implication linking Sir Oswald Mosley with extremists like Ramsay. A new regulation was immediately brought into force known as 18B(1A) which stated that members of 'hostile' organizations could now be arrested if they were 'likely to endanger' public safety, the prosecution of the war and the defence of the realm. These revitalized wide powers, entirely brought into being by the Kent/Wolkoff scandal, became law immediately. Sir John Anderson was defeated, and Mosley was arrested at his Dolphin Square flat, ironically only a few blocks away from Knight's office. Fifty-nine people were arrested in all, including Captain Ramsay.

For successful prosecution of Anna Wolkoff it was necessary to prove that she was an enemy agent, and this Knight did by using the Official Secrets Act. Although the Act covered both the acquisition and communication of secret documents, the defendant could be convicted only if the documents could be of use to an enemy and were communicated for a purpose that was prejudicial to the State. In 1920 a new Official Secrets Act stated that the defendant could be convicted if communication or attempts to communicate had been made with a foreign agent. In addition the agent need not necessarily be foreign by birth but only to have committed an act that was prejudicial 'to the safety or interests of the State'. Naturally the introduction of this act had made prosecution and conviction rather easier than before.

Sir William Jowitt, the Solicitor-General, who prosecuted both Kent and Anna Wolkoff, later stated that to convict them he had to prove that when Anna received the document she was acting as a 'foreign agent', for there was no concrete evidence that she had passed anything to Maringliano. Joan Miller, however, was able to report that Anna had said she was able to send material out of the country by the Italian diplomatic bag. When Anna had handed Joan the letter addressed to Herr W. B. Joyce, Rundfunkhaus, Berlin – for Joan ostensibly to send via the Romanian diplomatic bag – she neatly fitted the foreign agent description, although her message to Joyce was not 'secret information' but more in the nature of amateur propaganda.

The Home Office then tried to have Kent deported, but this was refused for fear of a public trial in America that would clearly ruin Roosevelt's re-election chances. Anderson later told the Cabinet that in the report from the security services it had been stated that Kent had been 'in relations' with Wolkoff. Chamberlain added that Ramsay's Right Club had been involved in pro-German activities and secret subversive work, with the object of disorganizing the Home Front and sabotaging war policy. He also stated that Anna Wolkoff had 'means of communicating with persons in Germany'. The trap Knight had set up for the Right had been successfully sprung.

Although the trial on 20 May 1940 was held in camera, the transcript makes it evident that it was conducted with scrupulous thoroughness. Knight was carefully cross-examined over the methods he had used in raiding and searching Kent's flat – even down to some sticky-backed labels that Knight had used to identify the files discovered in Kent's possession.

The transcript of the trial, still retained by M.I.5 in this country, demonstrates some of the searching questions Knight was asked. For instance, in relation to the labels, Knight was asked how long they had been in his custody. Knight replied that they had been in the custody of the Crown ever since the date of the arrest.

Defence counsel, Healy, persisted, 'How long have they been in your personal custody?'

Knight firmly replied that 'They have been in my personal custody only between the time of the arrest and the time they were handed over to the police.'

'Not long enough to change their character in any way by their being in your custody?' asked Healy.

'No,' said Knight.

Healy then switched his questioning to the raid. 'When you went to the rooms of Mr. Tyler Kent and searched them was he present?'

'Yes.'

'And was he present on all the occasions when you actually conducted the search?'

'To the best of my knowledge, yes.'

'You said something about having to break in?'

'Yes.'

'Had you tried to get in without breaking in?'

'Yes.'

'And was there no answer?'

'No, Kent shouted out, "You can't come in."'

'Then you had to break in?'

'Yes.'

'As a matter of fact you did get in, although there was a reason, which perhaps might have explained his objection to your going in.' (Kent had been in bed with his girl-friend at the time of the raid.)

'Yes.'

'Is it right to say that from the time you did get in he did not offer any objection to your searching anywhere?'

'No, quite true.'

'Further than that, these documents which have been put before the Jury as very deadly documents, none of them were concealed in any way?'

'That is true.'

'He might have brought them back from the Embassy and just put them away to where he would put away any ordinary documents.'

'I thought it very unlikely, because there was a large body of them.'

'There was a large body – I am conceding that, but there was no attempt made to distribute or conceal them in any way to prevent them being discovered?'

'No.'

Healy then switched his questioning to the involvement of Anna Wolkoff, attempting to prove that she came from a respectable family and should be seen as a decent expatriate Russian rather than a Fascist agitator.

'Part of the evidence that has been opened against Kent is the position of Miss Wolkoff in this matter. I want to take Miss Wolkoff as she was before the war, and I will go back a little. It is right that her father was Admiral Wolkoff?'

'Yes.'

'A distinguished officer in the Czarist Navy.'

'He was in the Czarist Navy. I cannot speak as to the extent of his service.'

'At any rate, you are not suggesting that he had a bad character in the Czarist Navy?'

'No; I know nothing about it.'

'He was a refugee to this country from the Soviet regime?'

'Yes.'

'And he was living in a humble shop at the corner of Kings Road and Harrington Road?'

'Yes.'

'Where the best caviare in London can be brought?'

'Yes.'

'Was Miss Wolkoff associated with him in that business?'

'To a very small extent, I believe.'

'They were fairly well known, where not they, amongst those who knew Russia?'

'Yes.'

'For instance, there was a book published which enjoyed some circulation, *The Russia I Love*, in which they were spoken of in the highest and warmest terms.'

'I believe that is true.'

Healy again changed the thrust of his questioning, this time trying to make the point that the policies of the British Union of Fascists had never been considered dangerous until war broke out. He asked Knight, 'Is it right that in this country there is an organization that runs on more or less Fascist lines?'

'Yes.'

'And until very recently it was accepted as one of the ordinary political parties in this country?'

'I should say that was a very difficult question to answer.'

Knight was guarded, and Mr. Justice Tucker intervened, asking Knight, 'Would you call it an ordinary political party?'

Knight replied, 'Well, my Lord, I think so, speaking generally. Was there any reason why it should have been regarded as anything but one of the ordinary parties in the country until quite recently?'

Healy then continued, 'That is what I want you to tell me, because it might be wrong for me to tell you. At what date did your Department begin to regard the Fascist party in the country with suspicion, or anything of that sort? Is it right that no suspicion of that sort became in any way public until comparatively recently?'

'No, with great respect. I should have said that roughly from the time of the Italian–Abyssinian war the Fascist party in this country was regarded with very grave suspicion.'

'Was that so outside the political circles?'

'Yes. I think the matter was first raised in the House of Commons.'

'At any rate, a large number of people were recently interned largely because of their membership of the Fascist party?'

'Not entirely.' Knight was determined to stick to accuracy, particularly in the light of his investigations into Mosley and a pacifist named Ben Greene.

'No, but a great number of the Fascist party were interned?'

'Yes.'

'Would it be right to say that from the time the Fascist party were threatened was the first time the attention of the public was really actively drawn to the doctrine of the Fascist party?'

'No, I should dispute that.'

Healy, however, was not interested in further discussion: 'There is a matter I do not think we differ about very much.' Then he returned to Kent's statement and the trial continued.

On 5 November 1940, Roosevelt was re-elected President of the United States of America, beating Wendell Wilkie by five million votes. Two days later, the press were allowed into the Old Bailey for the first time to report the public sentencing of Kent and Anna Wolkoff. Both were found guilty under the Official Secrets Act, Kent on five counts, receiving seven years' imprisonment, and Anna Wolkoff on two charges.[8] She received

---

[8] Later press reports stated that Anna, horrified to see Joan Miller as principal prosecution witness, threatened to kill her, but this has been proved to be quite untrue.

ten years' imprisonment, the length of the sentence reflecting the fact that she had become a naturalized British subject in 1935.

In 1945 Kent was deported to America and released. His mother had waged a constant battle for his return, trying to get him tried under U.S. law, but, fairly obviously, her many letters to Roosevelt provoked little reaction. In June 1944, the news of Kent's imprisonment leaked out, followed by some details of the case. There was an immediate furore, but although Roosevelt's opponents had a brief field-day this was brought to a swift halt by former Ambassador Kennedy, who had endorsed Roosevelt at the very last minute in 1940. Fearful for his own position, Kennedy gave an interview to reporter Henry J. Taylor which coloured the situation and unfairly, quite fictitiously, discredited Kent. He said:

> Kent's reported friendliness with the Russian girl, Anna Wolkoff, had its place in his attitude but apparently she didn't have safe and regular channels into Germany. . . . But Kent used the Italian Embassy to reach Berlin. For the most part he passed on secrets out of England in the Italian diplomatic pouch. Italy, you recall, didn't enter the war until after Kent was arrested. If we had been at war I wouldn't have favoured turning Kent over to Scotland Yard or have sanctioned his imprisonment in England. I would have recommended that he be brought back to the United States and then shot.

This astonishing piece of character assassination and total fabrication of the facts in order to cover up the Churchill/ Roosevelt correspondence is matched only by another fictitious scenario which appears later in the interview with Taylor. Here, Kennedy states that on the night following Knight's discovery of the documents held by Kent he (Kennedy) telephoned the President in Washington, warning him that the secret code was now useless and that the Germans and Italians, and possibly the Japanese, had possessed full details of everything sent in and out of the White House and the State Department for the last eight months. Kennedy went on to claim that for some weeks during the fall of France, the United States Government had to close its confidential communications system and was out of private contact with American Embassies and legations everywhere. During this critical time no messages could be received by the President or any of the staff. He also claimed that this unprecedented situation lasted for some weeks until a new unbreakable code could be devised in Washington and taken by special couriers to all American outposts.

'Nobody "railroaded" Kent,' he continued. 'The British sentence that put him on the Isle of Wight for seven years was mild beyond measure. The only thing that saved Kent's life was that he was an American citizen and we were not yet at war.'

Apart from Kennedy's conjecture that Kent had sent out secret documents in the Italian diplomatic bag (he was in fact never accused of conspiracy with Wolkoff at his trial), the unbreakable codes in which the Churchill/Roosevelt letters were written was a fantasy. They had been transcribed in the Gray Code, which had been read with ease by the Germans and other foreign powers since 1918. Indeed, the code was so familiar to American diplomats and military personnel abroad that a senior consul in Shanghai made his retirement speech in Gray towards the end of the twenties.

Looking back on his activities in a *Newsnight* interview with Robert Harris in 1982, Kent still clung to his belief that the decision of the Allies to go to war with the Nazis was a mistake 'not just on the part of Britain but on the part of the United States'.

He went on to say that 'all we've done is put on the map a country, Soviet Russia, that had concentration camps ten, fifteen or twenty years before Hitler was ever even heard of. So when you start talking about the moral angle of this thing, you put yourself in a ridiculous situation when you've allied yourself with Soviet Russia, which is worse in every respect.'

Kent probably genuinely believes this now, for his Russian masters did little to recompense him for his years in prison, and he has spent the remainder of his life to date advocating right-wing policies and the advantages of health foods. He now lives in a Texan caravan park, seven miles from the Rio Grande and the Mexican border. In the *Newsnight* interview Kent made a final riposte:

'I had no moral compunction about what I did. I know that, being young at the time and inexperienced, I did some foolish things which led to my imprisonment in England, but insofar as being right is concerned, I know that I was right because of the results of what happened and the deterioration of the world position of the United States.'

As an ironic footnote, Knight discovered, just before the Kent/Wolkoff trials, that Anna's parents were working in the censorship department in Wormwood Scrubs, next door to M.I.5, Admiral Wolkoff having been recruited with his wife to read outgoing overseas mail. The Admiral was hurriedly sent to an internment camp while his wife returned to the tea-rooms.

Following her release in 1947, Anna Wolkoff returned to the tea-rooms. But when they closed on her father's death in the late forties, she moved to a Bohemian lodging house in Tite Street, Chelsea, owned by Felix Hope Nicholson. Adrian Liddell-Hart, another Tite Street resident, remembers her vividly: 'She was a very right-wing, strident lady, much given to fanatical hatred of the Jews and the communists. She had no money and I think Felix must have let her live in the very top flat at a peppercorn rent. Anna made a slender living out of dress-making and her flat, where I once dined off a fearsome spaghetti dish, reminded me of Miss Haversham's room in *Great Expectations*. It was trapped in time and full of junk. She told me that whilst she was in prison she had initiated a gardening scheme for women convicts because she considered they lazed their sentences away. Naturally she was put in charge of the scheme and I could imagine her as some kind of female commandant. But once in Tite Street, she rarely went out and only had a few faithful old friends. Then, surprisingly, in 1969, Anna went off to Spain with a friend and was killed in a car crash.'

CHAPTER SEVEN

PROFESSIONAL AND PRIVATE
INTRIGUE: 1940–1944

BETWEEN and beyond Knight's three big wartime cases –
Kent, Mosley and Greene – there were a number of smaller,
stranger cases and events. Some had world-wide ramifications
but did not fulfil their potential. Some of the personalities and
events, however, were to have a lasting effect on Knight's career
and life.

Any sort of social life was difficult enough during the war,
with everyone engaged in essential war work, with overtime,
fire-watching or air-raid warden duty at night, but for M.I.5
personnel there was the added complication of secrecy. Perhaps
this is why members of M.I.5 tended to frequent the same
parties and why Knight's friendship with the Wheatley family
flourished, so that he began to involve Wheatley in an increasing
number of adventures. Wheatley was already useful to Knight in
employing Friedl Gaertner, and Knight prevailed upon the
G.P.O., through Bill Younger, to lay a special telephone line to
the Wheatleys' air-raid shelter in case 'we had the misfortune to
become entombed'.[1]

Wheatley, however, was anxious to become more directly
involved with M.I.5. He did in fact know Kell personally, Kell
having assisted him with his biography of Marshal Voroshilov.

[1] *Drink and Ink.*

Nevertheless, Wheatley's hopes of actively joining M.I.5 were to be dashed, for Knight, always being careful to hold something back, even with friends, told him that 'no post suitable to [his] capabilities was open'.[2] Wheatley hoped that 'the time would surely come when I should be wanted, and perhaps quickly, for some post where my abilities could be used to best advantage'.[3] Knight reminded Wheatley that the war and the black-out had put an end to most normal forms of entertainment, and that thousands of people in camps, in hospitals, or at home would depend upon him to maintain his prolific output of thrillers. But Wheatley was not appeased until a year later, when he submitted his famous 'War Papers' to the War Office. In them he outlined various tactical defence strategies in case of German invasion, and the War Office took them very seriously.

Before Joyce fled to Germany late in August 1939, Wheatley had, by chance, received him as a guest at one of his numerous parties. He had been brought by W. H. Tayleur (a Fascist sympathizer) who had helped Wheatley with proof-reading for some years. Wheatley remembered that Joyce had talked a good deal about Germany and expressed his disappointment that his books were not published there. This, he said, was because in Wheatley's Duke de Richleau series of books one of the heroes, Simon Aron, was a Jew; but despite this Goering was a great fan and was anxious for Wheatley to come to Germany, preferably in Joyce's company, to meet the Nazi leaders.

When Knight raided Joyce's flat just after his escape to Germany he found that his departure had been so abrupt that he had not destroyed any of his papers. Among this abandoned material he found a file on Wheatley in which there were copies of various reports Joyce had sent to Germany. In one of these Joyce reported that, as Wheatley had a number of Jewish friends, he could present something of a problem; but apart from this he had great potential as an excellent collaborator after the invasion and would make a first-class *Gauleiter* for northwest London. This testimonial would have made Wheatley

[2] *Drink and Ink.*
[3] *Drink and Ink.*

suspect throughout the war, had his friendship with Knight not enabled the pair of them to laugh at it. Ben Greene was imprisoned for less.

Joyce was being watched very carefully by M.I.5, yet at this time Knight told Kell that he was not a danger and Kell reported: 'I should not think anything could occur to shake his basic patriotism. His code of personal honour is probably peculiar, but very rigid.' Knight made the mistake of dismissing Joyce as a crank when he should have realized that he was dealing with a man of guile and intelligence.

Born in New York of Irish parents, Joyce was taken back to Ireland at the age of three in 1909. He arrived in England in 1921 when he was fifteen, having suffered the British withdrawal from Ireland and resulting rampant poverty, which gave him strong ideas about the British Empire and the Bolshevik/Jewish conspiracy that was destroying it. A brilliant speaker, and one of the most interesting members of Mosley's movement, he joined the B.U.F. early in 1933.

Joyce was a man of extraordinary contrasts, linked by impassioned hatred. He had been a Black and Tan informer, gained a first-class honours degree in English literature at Birkbeck College in London, and could be both loving and generous, but he was fanatical in his right-wing views. While still a student he had acted as a British Fascist steward at a Conservative meeting in Lambeth in 1924, and he was held down by left-wing militants while a razor was placed in his mouth. His face had been slashed right up to his ear, leaving a hideous scar that was to be a symbol of his hatred all his life. For various reasons, Joyce always attributed this attack to Jews, thus redoubling his venom and, as in January 1934 in Chiswick, causing him to make comments like 'I don't regard Jews as a class, I regard them as a privileged misfortune. . . . The flower or weed of Israel shall never grow in ground fertilized by British blood!'

Having been made redundant by Mosley because of dwind-ling party funds (Joyce had been Director of Propaganda for the B.U.F. for a period), Joyce and Becket created the National

Socialist League. This was extremely anti-Mosley in nature and launched vitriolic verbal attacks on the B.U.F., seeing their own movement as a response to the revolutionary yearning of the people to cast off gross, sordid democratic materialism without having to put on the shackles of Marxist materialism, which would be identical with the chains cast off. Joyce added that friendship with Germany was vital, particularly as, 'if Germany needs help in hurling Orientals back to the Orient, she is entitled to receive it from those who prefer white manhood and government to any other.'

Becket, later secretary of the Duke of Bedford's People's Party, was interned in 1940, as were the majority of the members of the National Socialist League. Joyce escaped to Germany in August 1939 and, as Lord Haw-Haw, regularly broadcast anti-British propaganda.

In the autumn of 1939, Knight asked Wheatley to involve himself with M.I.5 affairs more directly by keeping under surveillance a Hungarian lady known as Vicki, who was believed to be an enemy agent. Wheatley had originally met her at a cocktail party and later Knight told him that she had married a peer shortly before the war and was at present living in Mayfair. Her husband, now an R.A.F. officer, was stationed in the country. Knight's reason for believing Vicki to be an enemy agent was that before the war she was said to have been the mistress of a wealthy Jewish armaments tycoon, who was now living on a neutral ship trading between England and the Continent. Knight further claimed that although he had enough evidence to hang the tycoon, M.I.5 had no power to have him arrested, even when he was in a British port. All that could be done was to keep a vigilant eye on Vicki and prevent her from passing information to her boy-friend. This somewhat unlikely story was presented to Wheatley in the usual authoritarian Knight style, but even if he found the connection rather far-fetched he accepted it as Vicki provided just the kind of Mata Hari touch that he needed for his thrillers. Accordingly, under the pretence of trying to find a publisher for her memoirs, Wheatley invited Vicki to his numerous cocktail parties. Her constant companion at these functions was a black-haired Hungarian baroness who was rumoured to be yet another Nazi agent. Wheatley nicknamed her 'the Black Baroness' and used her as a model for a character in the third of his Gregory Sallust spy thrillers.

Wheatley asked two other socialites, Charlie Birkin and Captain Bunny Tattersall, to keep an eye on the two suspect Hungarian ladies as well. Bunny, who had been 'Man about Town' for the *Daily Mail* and was now in the Inniskilling Dragoons, was particularly useful, for he knew everyone and went everywhere.

In December 1939 Vicki herself threw a party. Among the guests was the Turkish Ambassador, who told Wheatley that in his opinion Hitler would subjugate the French in the spring and then invade Britain. Wheatley countered his complacency by making up a story about the King and Government retiring to Canada with the Navy, and continuing the war from the outposts of the Empire. At the same time, he said, the Americans would also come to the rescue. With Russia waiting in the wings, Wheatley did not see how Hitler could possibly emerge victorious! This must have given the Ambassador food for thought. Among the milling guests were several members of M.I.5. Apart from Dennis and Joan Wheatley there was Bill Younger and his sister Diana, Friedl Gaertner, Bunny Tattersall, Knight himself, Charlie Birkin and several others. With such a high head-count of case officers, agents and contacts, there is little doubt that the mysterious Vicki was well watched.

The German-Jewish refugee, Harald Kurtz, round in face and body and nicknamed Porpoise by refugee relief worker Jocelyn Baber 'because of his antics in the bathroom', was one of Knight's agents at this time, before he was involved in a disastrous attempt to use him as an *agent provocateur* to Ben Greene. Kurtz was largely used to infiltrate internment camps in an attempt to uncover subversion. Jocelyn Ba⎯⎯ remembers that Knight had bugged a flat in which Kurtz, posing as a spy, was to interview a female Nazi. At this time bugging was so primitive that it involved Knight and two Special Branch colleagues hiding in the bathroom while the interview took place. To assist the cramped listeners, Kurtz was instructed to place himself and his suspect in specific areas of the room so that all the conversation could be heard by the silent listeners. The suspect brought with her a large bag and, when she opened it, Kurtz spotted a large revolver inside. Desperate to convey this information to Knight, Kurtz said in an over-loud, precise, if somewhat apprehensive voice: 'Do you always carry a gun? I shouldn't if I were you.' Knight signalled his Special Branch men to rush into the room. So great was their confused enthusiasm that they captured Kurtz as well as the Nazi spy.

By the late autumn of 1939 the police had listed 71,600 enemy aliens; each one of these had to be checked or investigated by M.I.5. Anna Wolkoff was known to be on visiting terms with the Harlips, a White Russian husband and wife photographic team who had come to Britain in 1937 and ran a fashionable photographic studio in New Bond Street. Knight asked Joan Miller to investigate the couple, with particular relation to the Wolkoff visits. The original idea had been for Joan to be photographed by the Harlips, but as the M.I.5 petty-cash box contained only three guineas, another approach had to be taken. Joan therefore went to Gregor Harlip's studio and rather pathetically stated that she wanted to have a portrait taken for her fiancé but she could only afford a small sum.

Harlip gallantly took more than twenty photographs of the lovely Joan and accepted the small fee. As the Harlips photographed royalty and politicians (such as Churchill), Knight considered them to be in an ideal position to conduct espionage, but after months of checking he found no evidence at all to connect them with any such activity.

While these small investigations were being carried out something happened which proved to be another turning-point in Knight's career. That was the sacking, by Churchill, of Vernon Kell, who had been Director of M.I.5 since its inception. He was dismissed on 25 May 1940, just after the Tyler Kent case and the trauma of 18B internments. There were various reasons for Kell's dismissal. The first was unjust and concerned the sinking of the *Royal Oak* by a German submarine at Scapa Flow on 14 October 1939. Altogether 834 lives were lost and, as it was rumoured that espionage had provided Germany with information about the movements of the ship, M.I.5 was unfairly blamed for not preventing the tragedy in the first place and for not tracking down those responsible. There was probably no espionage involved at all, as the Admiralty precautions against underwater attack at Scapa Flow were woefully inadequate.

In January 1940, a mysterious explosion wrecked a gunpowder factory at Waltham Abbey in Essex, killing three workmen. Sabotage was suspected and, unfortunately for Kell, the disaster occurred in Churchill's own constituency. Once again M.I.5 was blamed for not preventing the tragedy and then failing to find the culprit.

More specifically, the inadequacies of the arrangements at Wormwood Scrubs had made the British Security Service a laughing-stock. (Although the invaluable card indexes had been microfilmed and taken to a safe place, an incendiary bomb in November 1940 destroyed many of the orginals.)

Kell had also taken the unfortunate step of recruiting the notorious Brian Howard as a minor M.I.5 agent, with instructions to report back to Knight on Fascist sympathizers. Howard was not a key factor in Kell's dismissal but his activities did make M.I.5 look extremely foolish. Knight himself was considerably shaken by Howard's behaviour, but at the time found it so outrageous as to be absurd. Only later did he realize that this was yet another nail in Kell's coffin.

Howard was a homosexual aesthete, an associate of such distinguished figures as Harold Acton, W. H. Auden and

Harold Nicolson. He was partly Jewish; though he had been a promising poet, his talent burnt itself out at Oxford, where he went after Eton in the autumn of 1922. Lady Caroline Lamb called Byron, 'mad, bad and dangerous to know'. The description fitted Howard too. An aggressive exhibitionist, he would often physically attack those around him, particularly when he was drunk. Howard set out to shock, but his real ambition was to be an eminent literary figure. This he failed to achieve.

Evelyn Waugh took him as the model for Ambrose Silk in his novel, *Put Out More Flags* (published in 1942), representing him as a shallow intellectual with fashionable left-wing opinions, a homosexual with a preference for young Germans. Howard himself wrote a slim volume of poetry called *God Save The King* in the late twenties but his other claim to fame was that he took part in one of the more celebrated japes of the time when he colluded with Brian and Diana Guinness (later Diana Mosley) in their presentation of a spoof private exhibition of modern paintings by a supposed expatriate German poet called Bruno Hatt on 23 July 1929. Howard was responsible for the paintings.

Kell recruited Howard in early 1940 and Knight was horrified by his rake's progress. However would confide in anyone who would listen that he was an M.I.5 agent and, as the evening progressed, would often accuse them or their associates of being German spies. Kell had employed Howard because he wanted an infiltrator in the homosexual world to detect possible Fascist sympathizers in those circles, as well as among his upper-class friends and associates, but he had not bargained for Howard's eccentric approach. Unhappily, Knight found himself responsible for briefing Howard, as he came under counter-subversion. Gradually Howard became involved in more and more situations which made him a dangerously notorious figure. On one occasion in the Gargoyle night-club he hit Guy Burgess for refusing to stand up for the national anthem (in fact he was too drunk to do so). This particular anecdote is supplied by a War Office employee, Mrs. Marie-Jacqueline Lancaster, from whose legs Dylan Thomas licked leg-paint (stockings were scarce) in time to the music. It must have been a memorable evening.

Acton wrote in *More Memoirs of an Aesthete*[4] that

Apparently members of the Secret Service enjoyed a special
licence to misbehave; there was always some hidden
motive as an excuse. Brian spoke of working for M.I.5 as if
he had joined some exclusive club. . . . There was an
obvious current of sympathy between Burgess and Brian,
who fulminated against rentiers and money men in his
latest role, but at bottom he remained a hedonist and a
snob. He had a heart, however . . .

In the reorganization following Kell's departure, Howard was
dismissed, much to Knight's relief, for whatever his personal
feelings might have been, he was too much of a professional to
make allowances for Howard's damaging antics. Brian Howard
committed suicide in 1958.

In addition to all these problems, Kell, now sixty-six, a
chronic asthmatic, was certainly not considered the right man to
lead M.I.5 during a Second World War. He was also a victim of
the manipulation of Sir Joseph Ball, Deputy Chairman of the
Security Executive, who wanted his own man, Brigadier A.
Harker, in the job. Unfortunately, and most damagingly, Kell
had not co-operated with Churchill sufficiently. He had been
deeply suspicious of him ever since Churchill had tried to merge
M.I.5 with the S.I.S. in 1915 and there had been a total
breakdown of communication between the two men. Indeed,
Desmond Morton, Churchill's private secretary, was now going
direct to Knight for situation reports rather than speaking to
Kell himself.

In the end, of course, it was not difficult to force his
departure, for Kell's age, poor health, and old-fashioned views
told against him. Kell took the news badly. On 26 May Lady
Kell, who ran the canteen at Wormwood Scrubs, called her staff
together and said: 'Your precious Winston has sacked the
General,' and Kell bleakly recorded in his diary on Monday

[4] (Methuen, 1970).

10 June 1940: '*Scrubs*. I get the sack from Horace Wilson 1909–1940. Italy comes into the war against us. Dirty dogs.' The next day he wrote: '*Scrubs*. I make certain farewells. I lunch Swinton[5] at Naval and Military Club.'

Knight, protected from the chaos at the Scrubs by his isolation at Dolphin Square, would probably have been sacked as well for being one of Kell's men, but because of his success with Kent and Wolkoff he was riding high and the ramifications of the Ben Greene scandal came too late to shake his position, although his reputation and credibility suffered.

On Kell's departure Churchill reorganized M.I.5 by imposing over it the Security Executive section of his Home Defence Executive. Chaired by Lord Swinton, with Sir Joseph Ball as Deputy Chairman, the members of the Security Executive included Kenneth Diplock, Brigadier A. Harker (as acting Director-General), Sir Alan Hunter, Colonel Roger Reynolds, Arthur Hutchinson, Edwin Herbert, Isaac Foot and Malcolm Frost (seconded from the B.B.C.).

Frost has told me that Swinton was put in to clear up one hell of a mess. Certainly considerable spring-cleaning was required and it was fortunate that Knight was so much out on a limb, 'unique in his own little set-up'. Frost also recollected that Knight got a kick out of what he did and thoroughly enjoyed intrigue. In preliminary meetings, during the early stages of the reorganization, he told Frost that there were homosexuals in M.I.5 and referred to them as the 'Homintern'. Subsequently, Frost met Blunt, whom he found 'intellectually arrogant'.

'As to Knight, I found him an enigma – for he had few friends outside the Dolphin Square office and it was almost impossible to get near him.'

He had an outer shell that was very polished, Frost discovered, so diamond-hard that it seemed impossible even to guess at what kind of person really lay beneath.

Screened from the brunt of Swinton's reorganization,

---

[5] Lord Swinton, Chairman of the Security Executive, who was responsible for reorganizing M.I.5 after Kell's departure.

Knight's case officers at Dolphin Square still consisted of Bingham, Himsworth, Brocklehurst, Gillson, Land, Poston and Younger. Bill Younger's sister Diana was a filing clerk there, although she was later to join the Special Operations Executive and claimed to have been dropped by parachute into France. John Bingham, later to become a distinguished writer of detective and spy stories, wrote in the foreword to his book *The Double Agent*:[6] 'There are currently two schools of thought about our Intelligence Services. One school is convinced that they are staffed by murderous, powerful, double-crossing cynics, the other that the taxpayer is supporting a collection of bumbling, broken-down lay-abouts.'

Knight's office in Dolphin Square was a far cry from both. Bingham has told me: 'Max was a wonderful leader and we were all devoted to him. In fact we adored him for he made serious work great fun – a unique quality. He gave tremendous support to the agents and he really cared about them as people.'

Bingham knew that Knight's interest in wildlife was vitally important to him and everyone in the Dolphin Square office was captivated by his enthusiasm.

'He always had something alive in his pocket,' said Bingham. 'You never quite knew what.'

Joan, however, was not a popular figure.

'She completely dominated Max,' Bingham told me, 'and she quickly became a person of considerable influence. I know we were all slightly afraid of her for we only needed to get on her wrong side and she would put the boot in for us with Max.'

In spite of Joan, Bingham had the highest respect for Knight and looks back on B5(b) with great affection.

'When the bombs came, Max clucked round like a mother hen for he regarded us as his family.'

Bingham also remembered that the popular image of M.I.5 personnel was that of tall, keen, hawk-eyed men.

'But we were all of different shapes and sizes – Max with his enormous nose and Bill Younger who was very short. We used

[6] (Dutton, 1967).

to call ourselves Knight's Black Agents after the passage from *Macbeth*:

Good things of day begin to droop and drowse,
Whiles night's black agents to their preys do rouse.'

Bingham later used that phrase as a book title, taking care to spell night the Shakespearian way.

Knight's relationship with Churchill's private secretary, Desmond Morton, was a key factor in his strength and independence. Later, while serving on the Joint Planning Staff in 1940, Dennis Wheatley also came to know him, and he remained a personal friend of Morton's for many years after the war.

Born in 1891, Desmond Morton was educated at Eton and the Royal Military Academy at Woolwich, joining the Royal Horse and Royal Field Artillery in 1911. He was severely wounded at Arras, and became Field-Marshal Haig's aide-de-camp. As Minister of Munitions from July 1917, Churchill frequently visited the front and was shown around by Morton. Writing in the second volume of his Second World War memoirs, *Their Finest Hour*, Churchill said:

I formed a great regard and friendship for this brilliant and gallant officer and, in 1919, when I became Secretary of State for War and Air, I appointed him to a key position in the intelligence, which he held for many years. . . . He obtained from the Prime Minister, Mr. MacDonald, permission to talk freely to me and keep me well informed. He became, and continued during the war to be, one of my most intimate advisers 'till our final victory was won.

Morton consulted Knight over all counter-subversion and counter-intelligence matters. He was unmarried, a staunch Catholic and an extremely intelligent and perceptive individual, who had worked for the Secret Intelligence Service in the 1920s.

8 Maxwell Knight in 1940, characteristically wearing a uniform to which he was not officially entitled. *(From the estate of the late Joan Miller)*

9 Major General Sir Vernon Kell *(left)*, Director General of M.I.5 from 1925 to 1940, and military companion. *(S & G Press)*

10   John Buchan, later Lord Tweedsmuir, was Press Liaison Officer for M.I.5 in 1917, eight years before Knight joined. *Greenmantle* and its successors certainly influenced Knight's own crime novels and may have helped inspire the sense of mystery he cultivated himself. *(Popperfoto)*

11   Knight as country gentleman. His rapport with animals extended beyond dogs to snakes, birds, bush-babies and parrots. He kept a large menagerie, and his pockets frequently held live insects or mice. *(Private collection)*

12   Olga Gray, Knight's first, highly successful, woman agent. Gray infiltrated the Communist Party of Great Britain in the autumn of 1931,
discovering and, at considerable personal risk, then exposing their spying
activities. Her efforts culminated in the Woolwich Arsenal spy trial in
March 1938. (*Private collection*)

13 Percy Glading, Communist spy-master, for whom Olga Gray kept a 'safe' house, was sentenced at the Old Bailey in 1938. *(Keystone)*

14 Sir Oswald Mosley in full cry at King's Hall, Stoke, in 1934. Knight played a major part in his internment in 1940. *(Popperfoto)*

15 *(Left)* Joan Miller, Knight's second woman agent. Beautiful, determined and resourceful, Miller infiltrated Fascist circles, among other things providing crucial evidence in the Anna Wolkoff/ Tyler Kent trial at the Old Bailey in 1940. Much feared and reviled by Knight's colleagues, she spent a disastrous period living with him in a safe house in Camberley. *(From the estate of the late Joan Miller)*

16 *(Right)* Anna Wolkoff, a Russian expatriate, fanatical pro-Nazi and fellow conspirator of Tyler Kent. She became friendly with Joan Miller, who had been sent by Knight to the Russian tea-rooms in South Kensington then owned by Anna's father. *(Keystone)*

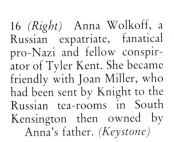

17 *(Above left)* The eccentric and sinister patriot Captain Archibald H. M. Ramsay, shown here at the Eton and Harrow match in 1937 with his wife Ismay. Knight infiltrated his Fascist Right Club and discovered that he was aiding Kent and Wolkoff. Ramsay was interned under Regulation 18B in 1940. *(BBC Hulton Picture Library)* 18 *(Above right)* U.S. Embassy official Tyler Kent. After exposure by Knight, Kent was sentenced at the Old Bailey to seven years in a British prison for stealing secret diplomatic documents. He was deported in 1945 after serving five years of his sentence, and is shown here arriving home in America. *(Keystone)* 19 *(Left)* One of Knight's secret memoranda concerning the documents found in Tyler Kent's possession. *(Private collection)*

20 *(Left)* Ian Fleming, creator of James Bond, who modelled Bond's boss 'M' on an amalgam of Maxwell Knight and his own boss in the Naval Intelligence Department, Admiral John Godfrey. *(Camera Press)*

21 *(Right)* John Bingham (later Lord Clanmorris), brilliant thriller and detective story writer and a member of Knight's exclusive B5(b) department in Dolphin Square during World War II. He is reputed to be one of John Le Carré's models for George Smiley. *(Private collection)*

22 *(Right)* Dennis Wheatley, thriller writer and Knight's closest friend. Wheatley had been a cadet on the *Worcester* and subsequently shared Knight's interest in black magic and involvement with Aleister Crowley – as well as his clandestine life in M.I.5. *(BBC Hulton Picture Library)*

23 *(Left)* Yet another literary man: Bill Younger, stepson of Dennis Wheatley, was one of Knight's closest aides at B5(b). He later wrote detective stories under the happy pseudonym of William Mole. *(Private collection)*

24 Possibly the most damaging of Knight's mistakes: Ben Greene, pacifist, Quaker, refugee worker, was wrongfully interned under Regulation 18B as a result of false evidence from Knight's *agent-provocateur*, Harald Kurtz. *(Private collection)*

25 *(Right)* Tom Driberg, 'William Hickey' of the *Daily Express*, and one of Knight's agents in the Communist Party of Great Britain. Driberg was expelled from the Party in 1941 following a tip-off by Communist agent Anthony Blunt. He is shown here electioneering after the war at the outset of his long political career. *(BBC Hulton Picture Library)*

26 *(Left)* William Joyce (later Lord Haw-Haw) captured in 1945, and another of Knight's mistakes: Joyce slipped through M.I.5's net in 1939 and broadcast anti-British propaganda from Germany for the rest of the war. *(Popperfoto)*

27　After retiring from M.I.5, Knight began a second career as a naturalist on radio and television. He rapidly became a household name in the fifties and early sixties and was especially popular with children. *(Private collection)*

He was also one of those responsible for creating the Industrial Intelligence Centre, whose job it was to report on industrial development in European countries, with an emphasis on the manufacture of armaments. By the mid-1930s the I.I.C. was looking carefully and apprehensively at the situation in Germany, where preparations were being made for the large-scale production of weapons, aircraft and tanks, easily outstripping British potential.

This information was not popular with Baldwin or Chamberlain because of their appeasement policies, but it was of essential strategic importance to Churchill. Indeed, without Morton's continuous briefings it is unlikely that Churchill would have been so well prepared to grasp at the power he wanted.

The S.I.S. (later M.I.6) was the organization that had wanted to take over M.I.5 between 1915 and 1927, the plan that Kell had fought against so strongly. Morton had watched closely the ramifications of Communist and Nazi subversion in the Olga Gray and the Tyler Kent cases, and he had been briefed by Knight on both so that he, in his turn, could pass the information on to Churchill. Naturally, this hot line to Churchill gave Knight substantial power and because of it Kell's successor, Petrie, continued to allow autonomy to Knight's Dolphin Square office.

Morton, because of his intelligence work, was as secretive as Knight, never publishing and even destroying all his private papers – a disaster for historians. After the war, he wanted to be forgotten, devoting himself to charity work, theological discussion and anonymous advice, in particular to the historian R. W. Thompson, who published some of their correspondence after Morton's death in August 1971.

Early in 1940, Joan became involved in surveillance of the lawyer Rajani Palme Dutt, who was a leading member of the Communist Party of Great Britain. Rajani Palme Dutt and his brother Clemens were the sons of an Indian doctor practising in Cambridge. Rajani had been expelled from Oxford during the

First World War for propagating subversive views. His brother Clemens became a Comintern agent in Paris and India, returning to specialize in converting students to the Party when he founded the first Communist cell in Cambridge in 1931. Both brothers were luminaries of the C.P.G.B.'s headquarters in King Street and had been watched carefully by Knight's office for some years.

Knight had intercepted a telephone conversation indicating that Palme Dutt kept some compromising documents in a locked steel trunk under his bed. Because Joan found befriending a leading Communist more difficult than dealing with the eccentric Anna Wolkoff, Knight decided that she should resort to more direct methods and break into Palme Dutt's flat to see what she could find in the steel trunk under his bed. To give her criminal expertise, Knight arranged for her to have police lessons in burglary. He had already provided her with a small gun and a leather-covered cosh, lined with lead, supplied by Swaine Adeney and Brigg in Piccadilly. Although these weapons were partly for Joan's protection they were also part of the fantasy game that Knight was beginning to play with her. Increasingly conscious of the failure of his marriage, he needed to find another female prop who would admire and believe in him.

The independent Lois, cut off and lonely, was beginning to look around for some war work that would not only screen her from Knight's indifference, but commit her to an absorbing life in which she would feel needed. Enid, still living in Putney, was regularly visited by Knight but also, separately, by Lois, who found in her a solid anchor in a vacuous world. The friendship of the St. Johnstons was also a support to her.

Once trained, Joan was told to attempt to break in to the Palme Dutt flat. Unwilling to go on her own, she persuaded Guy Poston to join in the escapade. Together they made a successful daylight entry by picking the Yale lock and, crawling under the bed as instructed, they found the deed box, protected by a seal. Breaking that open they discovered the box was empty except for a faded copy of a 1924 marriage certificate. After searching the flat for anything that might be important they were forced to admit there was nothing and they left, suffering from a great sense of anti-climax.

Another female agent of Knight's was Vera de Cottani-Chalbur. Her background was Russian, and she had worked for him from 1937 until the outbreak of war, based in a fashionable Mayfair salon and passing on scraps of information concerning potential Fascist sympathizers. Vera did not produce information of any great importance, but she was both intelligent and useful. Her value apparently came to an end at the outbreak of hostilities and she disappeared.

Knight next heard of Vera when he was contacted on 30 September 1940, by Peter Perfect, the Regional Security Liaison Officer in Edinburgh. Perfect told Knight that two damp, suspicious characters had been detained in a small fishing community on the Moray Firth. When searched by police they were revealed to be carrying equipment, a 6.35 Mauser automatic and two national registration cards showing addresses at 18 Sussex Place, London, W.11 and 15 Sussex Gardens, London, W.2. The two bedraggled suspects claimed their names were François de Deeker, a French refugee from Belgium, and Vera Erikson, an attractive young Dane. When asked how they had arrived in such an unlikely place, they stated they had landed from the *Norstar*, a ship reputed to be based in the Norwegian port of Bergen, that they had passed the night in a hotel in Banff, on the Firth, and had then taken a taxi to Portgordon.

Local police still found it difficult to account for their wet clothes and, in particular, for their interesting possessions. A search of the local area produced a pair of foreign-made Wellington boots on a beach at Gollachy Burn. Railway staff reported seeing a stranger buying a ticket to Edinburgh. A full-scale search in Edinburgh revealed a damp suitcase at the left luggage office and a few hours later police arrested its owner, from whom they took a loaded Mauser automatic and a flick-knife. Meanwhile, under questioning in Buckie, Vera Erikson dramatically revealed that she was, in fact, Vera de Cottani-

Chalbur and that 'Captain King' would vouch for her in London's War Office. She told Perfect that she was being paid by the Abwehr to guide two of its agents, Karl Drüke (later revealed to be François de Deeker) and Werner Wälti (the man arrested in Edinburgh) to London.

Knight admitted knowledge of Vera but merely stated that she had worked as an informer for M.I.5 before the war. He did not say that he had carefully prepared her as a double agent so that she would be able to trap Abwehr agents, just as she had now done.

Wälti, under interrogation at police headquarters in Edinburgh, also had a number of incriminating items on him, including a list of thirty-four airfields in the east of England and a wireless code. But despite all this, he stuck to a firm denial, claiming that he was Swiss, with a passport issued in Zurich, and had no knowledge of Drüke alias Deeker or Cottani-Chalbur alias Erikson.

Vera continued to give more details about the Abwehr, all of which were of vital importance to British security, and she was still passing information to Knight when she was later interned in Holloway.

Nine months later Wälti and Drüke, who had come ashore with Vera in a rubber dinghy, were tried at the Old Bailey and sentenced to death. Their appeal was rejected on 21 July 1941 and they were hanged at Wandsworth Prison on 6 August 1941. The press carried the story after the hanging (the trial was held in camera), but there was no mention of the part that Knight's double agent, Vera de Cottani-Chalbur, had played.

German espionage was not normally Knight's responsibility, but his previous use of Cottani-Chalbur, and his idea of using her as a double agent was the reason for his involvement on this occasion. Normally speaking, he concentrated on counter-subversion, leaving Liddell, Dick White, Jack Curry and Tom Robertson to cope with counter-espionage.

In September 1940 Knight decided that the double pressure of life with Lois and M.I.5 could be alleviated if he created a bolt-hole for himself combined with a safe house for agents. He decided that the pine-belt military town of Camberley in Surrey would be as good a place as any and he sent Joan Miller to do a reconnaissance. By this stage Knight was finding that his need for her was increasing and, under the pretext of a business trip, he would often take Joan into the country, where she gradually came to understand his absorbing passion for the animal world. With his M.I.5 cloak-and-dagger persona stripped away, he would show her wild flowers and small animals, handling them with such gentleness and humility that she could hardly believe that he was the same person.

Eventually Joan rented a secluded house in Camberley where she employed a maid and acted as a hostess. The cover story was that Knight was something in the War Office and that she, Joan, was his assistant on a strictly war-work basis. A youngish ex-guardsman called Potts was employed to drive Joan, Knight and their incognito house guests to and from London. Potts's wife had recently left him and he played a batman role to Knight, who enjoyed the company of a respectful servant. He would not have been able to afford such a figure in peace-time and found the arrangement most convenient. He would take Potts off for long fishing expeditions, at first with a new girl-friend Potts had acquired and later alone.

Joan was now very much in love with Knight and, although busy with M.I.5 tasks, still wanted to spend as much time as she could alone with him. But, like Gwladys and Lois, she found Knight elusive. He wanted her around but not always with him. But Joan was a stronger character than her predecessors, with far more driving force; she was not prepared to take second place to anyone – even Potts.

Just as she was about to remonstrate with Knight for what she considered too many outings with the boys, Joan received a nasty shock which quickly led to a creeping awareness of the real problem. Opening Knight's mail one morning, she found a desperate letter from Potts's girl-friend complaining that she was pregnant and that Potts was not allowed to see her because of his job. She wanted Knight to intercede and to send Potts back to her.

Knight was extremely shaken when Joan showed him the letter and she began to wonder not only why he had been going on so many fishing trips alone with his chauffeur but also why she had not yet been able to prevail upon him to sleep with her. Joan, although normally abiding by the moral rules of the times, would dearly have liked to have broken them in Knight's case, whether he was married or not. Yet he had given her no encouragement at all and, previously, Joan had assumed that he was either protecting her virginity or was still determined to be faithful to his much neglected second wife. Now, after reading this letter, Joan felt disturbed and puzzled, unable to understand why Knight had forbidden Potts his love-life and appeared to spend too much time in the man's company. She did not have to wonder long. Telling her that Potts had become a security risk, Knight summarily dismissed him.

The bombing of London began in September 1940. When an incendiary bomb damaged M.I.5's headquarters at Wormwood Scrubs, it was decided to move the bulk of the departments to Blenheim Palace at Woodstock. Eric St. Johnston, then Chief Constable of Oxfordshire, remembers that Malcolm Cumming, at that time Assistant Director of A Division – M.I.5's administration which included the Registry – asked him if he would lend him twelve policemen to move the secret files. St. Johnston agreed and once again ran into Knight, who told him that he and Lois had decided she should be evacuated to the country. As St. Johnston was looking for a secretary at the time, he asked her whether she would like to work for him in Oxfordshire. So from the autumn of 1940, for two years or more, Lois worked at police headquarters in Oxford while Knight continued to live in London. Knight visited Lois from time to time and, when he did, they stayed with the St. Johnstons. On this basis, Lois had practically no time alone with Knight and no knowledge of his relationship with Joan.

He had reverted to exactly the same relationship with Lois as he had established with Gwladys – a husband who was busy in London and could only spare time to see his wife occasionally. But in actual fact he was busy in Camberley with Joan, although here too he was able to absent himself on urgent business when he felt the relationship might become a sexual one with all the humiliation that might follow.

Early in the summer of 1940 Knight became interested in Krishna Menon, the left-wing Indian nationalist, who was of great importance to the Indian nationalist movement. He asked Joan to get to know him. She did as she was told but, because of a personal antipathy to Menon, she knew that she was not making the right kind of headway. One of the reasons for her success in the Tyler Kent case had been that she had liked Anna Wolkoff and had won her trust. Knight asked Joan to sleep with Menon, but she refused. She was replaced by a Belgian girl, Helen, who had done some work on the Kent case. A former drug addict, Helen was already having an affair with one of Knight's case officers, but she was more successful than Joan with Menon, who trusted her but revealed little of importance to M.I.5. Eventually Helen reverted to her drug dependence, entered a clinic to be cured, and later resumed work under a new case officer.

Joan returned to hostessing at Camberley, but this time there was a difference, for the closer she came to Knight as a person the more physically unobtainable he seemed to become. He still bought her lavish presents, kissed her and complimented her, but there was nothing more and she now felt his elusiveness becoming a wall between them. Joan was used to being successful with men, and she was puzzled by the fact that Knight wanted her only as a companion. In retrospect, she was both angry and defensive on the subject. She talks, for instance, of her suspicions of latent homosexuality being aroused when she met him by chance in a cinema café, avidly watching attractive young men. She also states that, on another occasion, having developed a passion for motor cycles (he even bought Joan one), Knight advertised for a mechanic and spent hours each weekend with him in the garden shed at Camberley. According to Joan, she saw him leave the shed one day, thinking himself unobserved, walking in a decidedly effeminate manner. The curious image this conjures up is too ludicrous to be really convincing but she is right when she says that Knight liked the company of young men, for Lois was also troubled by this tendency.

Ian Fleming, then in the Department of Naval Intelligence, was fascinated by Knight's mysterious persona, and was to involve him in an extraordinary adventure whose components – The Link, Aleister Crowley and Hess – were to make an explosive mixture. Years later, when Fleming wrote the first of his James Bond books, he used an amalgam of Knight and his own superior, Rear-Admiral John Godfrey, as the model for M, Bond's boss.

Recruited from a merchant bank to the D.N.I. at the beginning of the war, Fleming had a reputation for indolence and eccentricity that, in fact, masked a lively imagination and an analytical mind. Mainly restricted to work at a desk, Fleming's expeditions into the field were marked by a verve that staggered, and alarmed, many of his senior officers.

Rear-Admiral John Godfrey, who became Director of Naval Intelligence in 1939, had an extremely low opinion of Knight, an antipathy that was whole-heartedly returned. Their mutual suspicion reached its peak when it was thought that Godfrey would head the S.I.S., replacing Admiral Sinclair, who had died in November 1939. Godfrey mistrusted Knight's independence and, although S.I.S. would have no direct control over him, Knight feared his influence. In the end, however, Godfrey did not get the job, being beaten to the post by Stewart Menzies, who had been Sinclair's deputy.

Ironically, Sir Barry Domvile, whose pro-German organization, The Link, had been the subject of Knight's investigations in 1938–39, and who had been interned in 1940 under Regulation 18B, had been Director of Naval Intelligence from 1927 to

1930. It was Domvile and The Link that gave Fleming a brilliant, if audacious, idea. Having gone to Knight and studied Domvile's file, he suggested it might be possible to lure one of the Nazi leaders to Britain if The Link could be reborn for the occasion. The two of them built up a fictitious picture of The Link being driven underground but still retaining a membership influential enough to overthrow the Churchill government and negotiate peace with Germany.

Fleming knew the conservative Godfrey would never accept such a risky idea, particularly as it had a strong chance of back-firing embarrassingly on its originators. Knight, however, had a record of success behind him and was prepared to run big risks, so it was to him that Fleming entrusted much of the planning. The isolation in Dolphin Square was an advantage and he could also bypass high-ranking M.I.5, S.I.S. and N.D.I. officers. Fleming knew, for instance, that Knight had been going over Kell's head to Desmond Morton for years.

The next step was to look for a gullible Nazi leader and, to Fleming, the best candidate seemed Hitler's deputy, Rudolph Hess, who was not only anxious for peace to prevent Germany taking on the onerous task of attacking Russia, but was a student of astrology and the occult. Knight's thoughts turned at once to Crowley. He had had him in mind for some time as a potential M.I.5 agent, but because of his eccentric personality he was considered just a little too much larger than life to be successful. Yet here was a top Nazi leader who believed in the occult and here was Crowley, the artful perpetrator of occult practices. Somewhere, Knight thought, there must be a link.

But, at first, it was felt that Crowley could not be used and a more subtle method was envisaged. Fleming briefed an astrol-oger, via a Swiss contact, also an agent, to infiltrate Hess's occult circles in Germany. This he successfully did, ensuring that Hess was given the picture he and Knight had conceived, that of an influential band of plotters who wished to bring down Churchill and the Government and negotiate peace with Germany. The message was passed to Hess via a fake horoscope.

Knight, while gathering adrenalin from the very nature of this incredibly amibitious ploy, must still have found it hard to believe in. If he had already experienced the unfortunate results of the Ben Greene affair he would definitely not have become involved. But, for the moment, the whole business was a madcap adventure, and this was Knight's forte. The infiltrations of Olga Gray and Joan Miller had worked superbly, so why not send an M.I.5 astrologer into the occult court of Rudolph Hess?

Crowley had put up some of his own mad-cap ideas about helping the war effort to Wheatley and Knight. These included a project that involved the dropping of occult literature on the Germans, but neither Wheatley nor Knight felt this would have any practical application. Another drawback to Crowley's possible involvement in the Hess operation was that the Germans already knew, via a German agent who had lived with Crowley in Berlin, that Crowley had been passing information on Communism in Europe to the S.I.S.

Knight was to have bitter regrets over his involvement in Fleming's escapade as his confidence was eroded by the Ben Greene case, and he hurriedly withdrew to the fringes as Hess's interest in astrology increased towards the end of 1940. Fleming, meanwhile, had plunged deeper and M.I.6 let it be known that the Duke of Hamilton would be sympathetically inclined towards meeting Hess as a peace negotiator. Once this had been relayed to Hess he was immediately impressed, and he was further encouraged, when Ernst Schulter-Strathaus, a friend of Hess's adviser, Professor Haushofer, and himself Hess's consultant on astrology and the occult, told him in January 1941 that on 10 May six planets in the sign of Taurus coincided with the full moon. This was to set the seal on the date of Hess's planned journey and he must have taken it, at least, as another good portent towards his anticipated meeting with the Duke of Hamilton. The details of his subsequent flight and capture are well known.

Once Hess was in captivity, M.I.5 and M.I.6 congratulated themselves on a brilliant coup (although it was badly handled as a propaganda weapon) and Knight breathed a sigh of relief. The incredible plan had worked, largely as a result of Fleming's persistence. Crowley still waited in the wings and Knight now had no intention of allowing him on stage. Fleming was not so cautious and he suggested to Godfrey that Crowley might see Hess in prison and try to extract information from him about the influence of astrology on the Nazi leaders. It could have produced some interesting results but Godfrey turned the idea down out of hand. Ruefully, Fleming wished he had taken the proposition to Knight, but as Knight was now so much more cautious, he would have been unlikely to have received co-operation from him either.

In the autumn of 1941 Joan met an old friend, Richard Darwell. He had recently been invalided out of the Marines, after single-handedly capturing the Reykjavik radio station in Iceland, and was doing some sporadic journalism. Darwell, a man of considerable talent but very much a playboy, was looking for a permanent job.

Darwell's Icelandic adventures illustrate his immense re-sourcefulness. Originally bound for southern Ireland in April 1940, Darwell and his companions were sent on new orders to German-occupied Iceland on H.M.S. *Belfast*. On arrival his job was to close down the international frequency at the radio station and, as there was no resistance at the quayside, Darwell took a taxi up to the station. There he found the German Consul rapidly burning papers – Darwell arrested him. He later discovered that the German submarine crew who should have fought off the Marines were all in a brothel, where they were easily captured.

Darwell's detachment stayed in Iceland for six weeks and then sailed back on the *Lancastria*, enjoying a gourmet menu. (The luxury liner was later sunk in the Bay of Biscay.) Eventually Darwell, who had been inoculated with some defective vaccine, became ill and left the service. He had recovered and was at a loose end when he met Joan, who introduced him to Knight as a potential recruit. After an interview, Darwell was taken on to the Dolphin Square staff.

'Max had been in M.I.5 for a long time and seemed to know everyone,' Darwell told me. 'I enjoyed working for him although I could never get that close to him – no-one could except Joan, who held a privileged position in the office. We used to call her the Sacred Cow. She had considerable personality.'

Darwell carried out a number of investigations for Knight, including a Communist-watching stay in Oxford and a trip to Leeds to look into the reasons behind the coal-miners' strike. He remembers that he was particularly impressed by the absence of bureaucratic red tape at Dolphin Square.

'We had very much a free hand to recruit anyone we thought might be useful,' he reflects. 'Fabian of the Yard was a great contact of Max's as was Desmond Morton, to whom he had direct access.'

Joan saw Darwell as an ally, for she was becoming increasingly unpopular at Dolphin Square because of her 'privileged position' and the fact that she was very obviously, in name at least, Knight's mistress. By now, in 1942, Joan was also conscious that Knight was not so popular with M.I.5's top management, although his leadership qualities remained as strong as ever. The fact that he was difficult to understand, his direct line to Churchill via Morton, and his crude use of Kurtz and others in the Ben Greene case, did little to improve his popularity or status.

Harker, with whom Knight had a good relationship, lasted only a few months as Kell's successor; he was superseded, under the Security Executive's reorganization, by sixty-one-year-old David Petrie, who remained Director-General until 1946, with Harker as his deputy. Petrie's background was the Indian Political Intelligence Bureau, where he had been Director, so he was very experienced in intelligence work. He frankly regarded Knight as a has-been, a man from the old Kell administration, and but for the war he would have dismissed him. But Petrie also felt that B5(b), Knight's department, was still doing a vital job and should be left intact until the end of hostilities. Knight was highly protective over the Dolphin Square offices, for he knew that if he lost his isolation and his mystery he might also lose his job. So if any member of M.I.5 interfered with B5(b) under the Petrie organization, Knight would immediately phone Harker in high dudgeon to complain.

Although Knight was still occasionally visiting Lois in Oxfordshire, the marriage was to all intents at an end, although this fact did not emerge publicly until Lois went to Eric St. Johnston in considerable distress.

He recalls: 'Lois came to stay on her own and after dinner burst into tears and said that she and Max were separating. She then told us that throughout their marriage Max had been impotent and that their marriage had never been consummated.'

This was a great shock to the St. Johnstons. They found it difficult to give Lois advice, although they did their best to console her. The marriage was finally annulled in 1943 and Lois remained at the Oxfordshire Constabulary as St. Johnston's secretary until he joined the armed forces later in the year.

But despite Knight's relationship with Joan, the ending of the pale shadow of his marriage to Lois hurt him deeply. Once again it demonstrated his inadequacy, but he masked the impact of this by continuing to act as a mystery hero to Joan, though a flawed hero, from her point of view. His sister Enid was both shocked and worried, realizing that her brother's problems were increasing.

'I still thought there was somebody else,' Lois now reflects. 'If only he could have been honest with me – about everything – I'm sure we would have found the strength to face it together.' Apart from being distraught, she was very angry that Knight had been unable to face his problem, 'particularly when I had been thinking all the time it was my fault.' She knew that he needed women, that he had too much self-control yet wanted desperately to control others. She had been proud of his job, of his mysterious comings and goings, and she regretted the end of their marriage. 'He told me he wanted to find a doctor so that he could be helped, but I don't know if he ever went to see one.'

In all the legal details, the division of personal possessions and the final parting, Knight could not have been more kind and gentle to Lois.

'He would phone me to see if I was "all right" and, because time hung so heavy on my hands, I would still see Enid. But I still remember the most pure part of Max – the part that I shared – his love of the natural world.'

Joan also shared Knight's enthusiasm for the animal kingdom; he had given her a Great Dane and a Himalayan monkey who hated women. The period between late 1942 and early 1943 was one of increasing tension for Joan. Now that she had convinced herself that homosexuality was the reason for Knight's lack of physical passion, she felt that she had grown too close to him for comfort and, without any real evidence, she began to feel threatened by him. Knight had confided in her about his occult interests, and although she presumed this interest was academic, she was becoming frightened of his intuition. She began to believe that he knew exactly what she was thinking – which was probably not too difficult as Joan showed her emotions openly. A further aggravation was the fact that the Wheatleys, who often came to Camberley, did not like Joan and showed it, regarding her, no doubt, as an overbearing mistress. Gradually she convinced herself that Knight posed a physical threat to her and she came to be terrified of being alone with him, a situation that she had previously cherished. Seeking Darwell's support, she invited him down to Camberley with his new girl-friend, Babe Holt. But even when Darwell was there, Joan kept remembering how ruthless Knight could be and how she had heard gossip that he once employed a hit-man to get rid of unwanted people. Then something happened to increase her alarm. Knight had recently been discussing with Wheatley the possibilities of astral projection.[7] Glancing into Knight's bed-

---

[7] Many ancient religions or cults and some modern psychic researchers consider that the human form comprises two bodies, one physical and the other astral. The astral body is believed to be a perfect replica of the physical. The occult theory is that some people have learnt to detach the astral body from the physical one.

room one evening she thought she saw him standing by the window, yet still lying in his bed. Fantasy or not, it was a nightmare impression that stayed with Joan a long time. A few days later she told Knight that she was leaving him.

This was the first time that a woman acting as his wife had deserted him. He had let Gwladys and Lois go when he could no longer cope with their demands, but when Joan left him he had felt himself to be still in control. He took it very badly. Joan, too, was deeply unhappy, for all her sex appeal had been used on him in vain. They continued to work together uneasily at Dolphin Square.

In June 1943 Joan met and married a young naval officer. Naturally, this increased the tension between her and Knight. She was still afraid of him but, as they were no longer living together at Camberley (Knight was there on his own) her fears were partly relieved.

Because her job was classified it was not easy to get a transfer, but eventually she managed to find a post in the Political Intelligence department of the Foreign Office. There she read top-secret cables and arranged for their circulation to other departments, mainly to the Special Operations Executive or the deception planners at the War Office. But even here Joan could not shake off her contact with Knight, for, alerted by her espionage training, she noticed that one of her colleagues, a Major Bell, was taking an inordinate amount of time dealing with Foreign Office cables that related to the Middle East. She discovered that he was transcribing the information on to separate pieces of paper. Joan went to Knight, who investigated, eventually telling her that the phone tap on the C.P.G.B. headquarters in King Street was revealing details of the cables, as were his agents inside the building. Bell was later arrested with his notes in his pocket.

The final parting between Joan and Knight did not occur until 1945. It was very painful, for Joan then realized for the first time how much Knight had come to hate her. In the heyday of their relationship Joan claims that Knight had torn up a file he had been keeping on Richard Darwell because, prior to his relationship with Babe Holt, he had been seeing a girl who was considered a security risk. The destruction of such files was, of course, completely forbidden, but apparently Knight had enjoyed demonstrating his power to Joan. Now, she alleges, he was regretting it and, knowing Joan had lost faith in him, he seemed frightened that she might reveal his crime. Joan claims that over lunch in the Royal Court Hotel in Sloane Street he calmly threatened to blame her for destroying the file, telling her that, as he was much more powerful than she, no-one would ever believe her denials. She never saw him again.

CHAPTER EIGHT

RIDING FOR A FALL: 1940–1942

THE secret of Knight's success before the outbreak of war lay for the most part in the recruitment and handling of his women agents, notably Olga Gray and Joan Miller. Their work in the field was matched by his support and successful analysis of their findings and together they made a highly efficient team. This was not to be the case with his male agents, whose own aspirations and personality defects often obtruded, to the detriment of the highly taxing work on which they were engaged.

Counter-espionage obviously became vitally important as war drew closer, and it was essential that all potentially subversive organizations were infiltrated and as many suspect individuals as possible kept under surveillance. Knight and his case officers at Dolphin Square were therefore working under great pressure and did not in fact discover until later that some of the agents they had selected were not absolutely sound.

The rise of the extreme Right had been observed by M.I.5 with great disquiet from its inception, and although the Tyler Kent/Anna Wolkoff case was to provide ammunition which would devastate all right-wing organizations, in the early days it was obviously necessary to infiltrate a number of agents into key positions, in the hope that some of them would be able to provide evidence of treason.

Of all right-wing organizations the B.U.F., headed by the brilliant, charismatic Oswald Mosley, was the prime target, but unfortunately the agent Knight selected to infiltrate the party turned out to be extremely suspect. With hindsight it is easy to see why Knight made this particular error of judgement. Bill Allen, who had originally been a Conservative M.P. until he joined Mosley's New Party in 1931, was an old friend of Mosley and had married Paula Casa Maury, also a long-standing friend. He was therefore in an ideal position to keep Knight well informed on Mosley and the B.U.F. Allen was the managing director of a Northern Ireland printing firm which had strong financial contacts abroad. He was asked to receive sums of money destined for the B.U.F. from abroad, and reported back to Knight accordingly. Allen was also involved in a company called Air Time Ltd., which was financed by Mosley. Mosley wanted to set up a series of radio stations that between them would cover the entire country. They would be supported by advertising and would break the B.B.C.'s monopoly legally by being sited in the Channel Island of Sark,[1] the Irish Republic and Heligoland, which was German territory. This was to be a purely commercial rather than propagandist activity; Mosley hoped to make a fortune out of it to finance the B.U.F. He tried to interest Hitler in the scheme and his wife, Diana, made several trips to Germany, despite the fact that the Führer had turned down the idea in 1937. By 1938, however, she had managed to reawaken his interest and by 1939 Air Time Ltd. was about to be launched in Heligoland with profits split between the English company and Germany – only to be halted by war. Allen was able to report back the content of Diana's frequent visits to Hitler (which otherwise could have been misunderstood by M.I.5), thus giving Knight another reason for sending Robert Blockey from Haslemere Natural History Museum to Heligoland. Somewhat disarmingly, Mosley guessed that Allen was a mole, although he did little about it, and Nicholas Mosley writes: 'I have evidence from my father that he knew perfectly well that Bill Allen was working for M.I.5 at the same time as being one of his right-hand men. My father

[1] The Dame of Sark, who ruled the island, admired Mosley.

believed that Allen was a sort of Walter Mitty character and the accounts of conversations he gave to M.I.5 could have been partly fictitious. My father was extraordinarily insouciant about this. He did not seem to mind. He was a gambler.'[2]

Mosley himself was to say that Allen was 'very much involved with M.I.5, made no bones about it, that is why he wasn't imprisoned in the war, of course, because he had done so much for them.' But had he? The Walter Mitty side of Allen could easily have made him invent much of the information he supplied. M.I.5's claim and report (in June 1934) that Allen himself was regarded (by M.I.5) as a chief theorist of British Fascism and had 'influence on Sir Oswald', by its obvious inaccuracy diminishes Allen's effectiveness as an infiltrator. It is likely that Knight thought he would be able to turn Allen, making him that much more effective. But Knight's attempt failed, leaving Allen wallowing in megalomania.

The problem about M.I.5 reports on the B.U.F., revealed by documents declassified by the Home Office in November 1983, is that some of the evidence comes from the unreliable Allen. Nevertheless, it is clear that Knight had the B.U.F. under careful surveillance from 1934 onwards. Secret reports, with information supplied by Knight to Sir Vernon Kell, were sent to Sir Russell Scott, then Permanent Secretary at the Home Office, indicating the structure, expenditure and leading figures.

In 1934 Knight had been confident that the B.U.F. was fading out, largely through lack of funds. But he was concerned that industry, faced by the prospect of a Labour Government with a substantial nationalization programme, might decide to back the party. One of Kell's reports criticizes the *Manchester Guardian* for taking Mosley 'almost more seriously than he takes himself' and goes on to point out that the conditions that had led to the success of the Fascist movement in Italy and in Germany did not exist in England. Following the violent scenes at Olympia on 7 June 1934, Kell states, Mosley 'suffered a decisive check', adding that Dr. Robert Fegan, Mosley's deputy, who was shortly to

[2] *Beyond the Pale, Sir Oswald Mosley and Family 1933–1980* (Secker and Warburg, 1983).

resign, was beginning to have doubts as to his leader's sanity.

The source of funding of suspect organizations was obviously one of Knight's prime interests. In the case of the B.U.F. he had found it difficult to discover exactly who was providing the funds that were available. It was widely rumoured that Mussolini was providing £3,000 a month until 1936, but Mosley himself strenuously denied this. It is possible that Bill Allen might have been a go-between in such an arrangement, but, as this was the kind of role he loved to see himself in, it is difficult to state whether it existed outside his imagination. Other contributors, later revealed by Kell, included Lord Nuffield, the motor manufacturer, Lord Inchcape, the shipping tycoon, A. V. Roe, Baron Tollemache, Lord Lloyd, the Earl of Glasgow, Sir Charles Petrie, Vincent Vickers and Air Commodore Chamier of Vickers. Eventually the violence associated with the Fascist movement began to scare off potential backers and when Mosley was asked during his interrogation by Norman Birkett whether it would be possible to tell from his books whether Lord Rothermere had been a contributor, Mosley replied:

'No, certainly not.'

'Why?'

'For reasons I gathered, which I subsequently found to be true, that his advertisers threatened to boycott him, and that was why the *Daily Mail* stopped backing us, and the Jewish advertisers, Lyons and those sort of people. He was frightened out of his wits, most of these business men were. For instance, Lord Nuffield, as was common knowledge in the early days of our party, gave us large sums of money, but he even went so far as to publish in the *Jewish Chronicle* that he was not supporting us because his cars would have been subject to a boycott. I do not say that Nuffield supported us afterwards, but these men were at colossal pains to hide their connection with the movement; in fact, it was a joke among our people the lengths these people would go to conceal their connection.[3]

[3] Home Office documents compiled in the summer of 1940 and declassified in 1983 by Home Secretary Leon Brittan. Quotations throughout this chapter are from this source.

By 1936, however, Kell was reporting that M.I.5 had information from 'an absolutely reliable source' (the doubtful Allen) that Mussolini was now providing only £1,000 a month, but there was no evidence to show that Hitler was providing any funds. The Germans had in fact sent an agent named Colin Ross to England in April 1936 to enquire into the B.U.F. and, according to the Special Branch, he had reported back to Hitler that the movement had 'a fine policy and a splendid leader, but absolutely no organization'. Mosley would have been furious if he had known.

Meanwhile, Special Branch had revealed that the B.U.F. had a secret account at the Charing Cross branch of the Westminster Bank, which was used for laundering foreign funds. Mosley denied a detailed knowledge of the account, adding that he thought the funds came from well-known capitalists who were 'terrified of being found out . . . and they paid their subscriptions in foreign currencies.'

On 11 March 1935, Kell told the Home Office that 'According to one well-informed reporter from a quarter which we have no reason to distrust, "cells" have been successfully formed in various branches of the Civil Service.' This same report adds that 'some of the "cells" in the Civil Service are sufficiently high placed to enable National Headquarters to obtain information of important events before it is made public. No specific instances of this can, however, be quoted.' The Home Office then alerted the Prime Minister and the Head of the Civil Service and Knight's department was told to keep a special watch on the B.U.F.

Just before Mosley was interned, the Home Secretary, Sir John Anderson, reported to Churchill at the important Cabinet meeting of 22 May 1940, that he had a long talk with Knight and another M.I.5 officer (possibly Bill Younger) who had devoted special attention to the Fascist organization. Anderson pointed out that Knight had not been able 'to produce any evidence on which action could be based, showing that either the Leaders of the Organization or the Organization itself had anything to do with what might be called Fifth Column activities'. Knight had, however, told Anderson that certain members of the B.U.F. would be willing to go to any lengths. Still not convinced, Anderson informed Churchill that his own view was that Sir Oswald Mosley 'was too clever to put himself in the wrong by giving treasonable orders'. Anderson added, however, that he realized the War Cabinet might take the view that no risk at all should be run in Mosley's case. Mosley's blackshirt image, his original admiration of the Nazis and his anti-Semitism had long ago damned him in the eyes of the thinking – and the unthinking – public. Mosley was a liability the War Cabinet could not afford and owing to the damaging information supplied by the Kent/Wolkoff case he was interned a few days later. A man with enormous potential, a tragic figure, Mosley had in many ways damned himself, largely by his aloofness – and his certainty that only he was right.

While Mosley was in Brixton, angrily preparing the notes for his defence, Knight carefully monitored one of his secretaries as well as bugging his prison cell with concealed microphones. As a result, when Lord Birkett came to interrogate him he had already been told how Mosley would attempt to defend himself, the information being derived from 'a very secret and delicate source'. Knight and his department, in association with Graham Mitchell from M.I.5's F3, together with Bill Allen, were responsible for supplying the evidence against him.

Since Mosley's death in 1980 Diana Mosley has campaigned for the release of Norman Birkett's interrogation of her husband, which she claims should finally clear him of any treasonable intentions. This has now taken place, yet today, in 1983, she is still understandably dissatisfied by the continued retention by M.I.5 of six important files.[4] She told me 'Kit [as she called Mosley] was never embittered, but only maddened at the way England came bottom of every league.' She went on to say very emphatically that Mosley claimed the secret of success lay in the Empire, and when that was lost, he felt he had lost everything – unless a united Europe could be brought about.

'I was asked to lecture about him at a public school recently

[4] These concern Anthony Blunt.

and the man who introduced me to the boys later wrote an article asking why the Mosleys didn't feel guilty. Why should we feel guilty? We were right. . . . My sister, Unity, shot herself because she was so devastated that Britain and Germany were going to war. She lived for eight years afterwards but she was never the same again. I often think of my own imprisonment and how the press said Kit and I were living in luxury during the war. As we were locked up in a filthy gaol and Kit was dying from phlebitis it was a strange idea of luxury. I had been separated from Max [her youngest son], then a baby, when I was still breast-feeding him. I can still remember how I longed for him and for Alexander who was eighteen months when they took me away. . . . I've never had the slightest doubt that Kit was right. If a man is to be imprisoned without a trial, at least what he said should be made public.'

While there were some obvious reasons for Mosley's internment, the reasons for Ben Greene's internment were far more dubious and as a result Knight forfeited a good deal of his superiors' belief in his ability.

Once again Knight's choice of agent was extremely unfortunate. With Olga Gray and Joan Miller he had been able to rely on qualities of commitment and single-mindedness, and although Bill Allen was both unreliable and egocentric his was not the sole testimony against Mosley. With his next agent, Harald Kurtz, Knight discovered a devious personality, a trait he was unfortunately to use to its full advantage.

Kurtz was born in Germany in 1913 and was educated at the Adenwald Schule under a remarkable headmaster named Gebeb, who encouraged the parallel growth of mind and body, in much the same tradition as Kurt Hahn's Salem, which was later recreated in Britain as Gordonstoun. Kurtz was Jewish, homosexual and academically clever. Jocelyn Baber, a refugee relief worker in the thirties, knew him as a gifted and willing pupil 'who was probably our best known "pure Aryan" refugee', at least in appearance.

Kurtz arrived in Britain during the early thirties and worked at the B.B.C. as a translator. He always seemed to be short of money and was usually in debt, despite the fact that he was a distant relation of Queen Mary. Realizing that patriotism would be a useful commodity, he signed his letters with a crude drawing of a Union Jack. When Knight was introduced to him, he was struck by Kurtz's Aryan appearance. As a result, he seemed the ideal stool-pigeon, someone Knight could place in internment centres or camps to report on subversive influences. Kurtz became an M.I.5 agent, not because of his professed love of the Crown, or his hatred of the Nazis, but because he needed the money.

At first Kurtz was highly successful, enthusiastically denouncing at least a couple of dozen internees. But he went too far when he denounced Ben Greene, and the ramifications of the case were to have serious results for both Knight and himself.

Ben Greene was a member of a very large family of which Graham Greene, the novelist, Sir Hugh Carleton Greene and Felix Greene, the China-watcher and writer, are leading members. The family was based in Berkhamsted, where they were split into two – the School House[5] Greenes and the Hall Greenes. The Hall Greenes, of whom Ben was one, felt overshadowed by the more intellectual School House Greenes, epitomized by Graham and Hugh Carleton Greene, while they in turn felt detached from their richer cousins. In the first volume of his autobiography, *A Sort of Life*,[6] Graham Greene wrote:

At the far end of Berkhamsted at the Hall, the great house of the town, lived the family of Greene cousins. The mother was German and the whole family had an intimidating exotic air, for many of them had been born in Brazil, near Santos, on a *fazenda* which was also the name of the coffee we drank. There were six children, the same number as in our family, and in ages they were inserted

[5] At Berkhamsted School, where Charles Henry Greene was headmaster.
[6] (Bodley Head, 1971.)

between us, our family starting first, as though my Uncle, who was the younger brother, had suffered from a competitive spirit and wanted to catch my father up. My own particular friend was Tooter [Edward, Ben's brother]. ... My Uncle's children were the rich Greenes and we were regarded as the intellectual Greenes.

Ben Greene was born in Brazil in 1901 and came to England when he was ten. Much of his pacifist belief stemmed from his mother's attitude to her native land. She had been horrified by the Kaiser's arrogant militarism. Ben went to Berkhamsted School where, having grown to be extremely tall, he was deeply self-conscious and miserable. A shambling giant at fourteen, he was ostensibly an extrovert, but concealed a highly introverted personality dedicated to books and ideas. His idealism neverthe-less was of the highest. Graham Greene remembers him, none too kindly, as he recalls his own position as the headmaster's son. 'My cousin Ben, a junior prefect, one of the rich Greenes, worked covertly against my brother, gaining much popularity in consequence, so that I felt less sympathy for him when he was later imprisoned, without warrant or reason, in the second German war, under Regulation 18b. Injustice had bred injus-tice.'

Still at Berkhamsted, Ben Greene was nearly seventeen when the armistice of 11 November 1918, was signed and he shared with many an immense relief that German militarism had been halted. He firmly believed that a new age of peace and justice would begin and wrote in an unpublished memoir:

I felt the deepest admiration and gratitude to those who had sacrificed and suffered who had made this victory possible. But dominating all thought was the conviction that if this immense effort directed to destruction and death was possible, what could not be achieved if such an effort were directed to the construction of a new and just society. This thought has never left my mind, provided always that a permanent peace could be established.

At Oxford Greene joined the Society of Friends (Quakers) because he was convinced that organized Christianity had failed to face the moral issues which the First World War had produced. His first great disillusionment with the new age came when Greene realized 'with what brutal sneering and cold ingratitude the ex-service men were being treated' as they tried to adapt to civilian life with barely enough money to live on.

Greene's next disillusionment came when he was travelling in Germany for the first time while on vacation from Oxford. He was horrified by what he described as the 'treachery of the Peace Treaty'. Working for the Friends' Emergency Committee, doing relief work with students in Berlin and other parts of Germany, he realized the 'outraged bitterness' of every German at the duplicity of which they considered they were victims. Large sectors of the community had condemned the new democratic German Republic for having submitted to such terms and the passionate Greene was rightly certain that another war would occur unless the Peace Treaty was amended. The revised boundaries, the blame for the war, the appalling conditions – all made Greene offer his services to the Friends' Family Relief Committee to work in conjunction with the American Friends and American Relief Administration, organized by the U.S. Government to help in the severe famine that had begun in the Volga regions.

After leaving Oxford, Greene became Ramsay MacDonald's Private Secretary during the first Labour Government of 1924. By 1931, he had stood unsuccessfully as a Labour candidate for Gravesend, having inherited his father's wood-pulley factory in Berkhamsted, from which he was able to draw an income. Later in the 1930s he decided that the Labour Party had an undemocratic structure and this led him to create the Constituency Parties Movement which, by 1937, had brought about a radical reorganization in both the election methods and structure of the Labour Party National Executive Committee.

Despite his public work, at home his vivacious wife, Leslie, found him extremely anti-social, preferring to shut himself up in his study with his books. His son Paul, now running a successful tutoring establishment at Oxford, looks back on him with adoration: 'He was a remote father in the sense of personal contact and we were not allowed to play noisily when he was working, but he was also a deeply sensitive, loving person and we loved him dearly.'

Greene's progress towards internment had little to do with his political public life and was largely the result of his pacifist convictions. By 1935 he was a Deputy Returning Officer for the League of Nations plebiscite in the Saar. Soon his continued conviction that a lasting peace could not be maintained without a major revision to the Treaty of Versailles led to a rift with Ramsay MacDonald over the Geneva Protocol, and later still other rifts with Labour Party colleagues over the situation in Europe. Greene made repeated trips to Germany where, through the Quaker movement, he went to the aid of Jewish refugees. Nevertheless, he was insistent that there could be no justification for war with Germany and, just after the Munich agreement in 1938, he resigned from the Labour Party.

Feeling very strongly, if unimaginatively, that those who did not condemn the Nazis outright must secretly be for them, Knight was becoming increasingly uneasy about Greene. He was extremely outspoken and made no secret of his pacifism and the fact that he admired the socialist aspects of the Nazi movement, although he was very critical of the Nazi attitude towards the Jews. Knight already had him under surveillance but had been unable to find sufficient evidence against him. He therefore decided to try and discredit him by undermining his standing as a public figure and as a magistrate, a position which Greene had held for some years.

This was a drastic departure from Knight's usual methods, but the tension of the slow build-up to the outbreak of war was beginning to take its toll and M.I.5 was under increasing pressure to provide evidence against potential Nazi sympathizers. The following incidents were carefully recorded by Greene in an unpublished manuscript.

Passing through London rather late at night, Greene decided to stop and have a meal at a small café near Piccadilly. He parked his car in Berkeley Square and, walking to the café, noticed a woman who was behaving strangely. 'I noticed a woman who was trying to draw my attention to herself. She did not look like a prostitute but I ignored her and went into the café.' When Greene finally emerged she was standing on the opposite side of the street and, as he went over to his car, she called out his name and asked, in German, if she could speak to him. She gave Greene a name which he did not recognize and went on to explain that she had seen him in Amsterdam where she had been a secretary to the assistant of one of the refugee organizations, that she had also seen him at a refugee reception camp in Felixstowe and she herself was now a refugee. She claimed to have recognized him by his great height and said that the meeting was a coincidence. When asked why she was on the streets, she shrugged and said 'What can I do? If I didn't do as I was told I'd be finished.' The woman went on to say that no-one knew her in Britain and her disappearance would never be noticed, 'with her throat cut and her body disposed of'. Greene was not surprised at her story and considered it a classic example of what he had been trying to convey to the Home Office as one aspect of the refugee problem. The woman went on to explain that he couldn't help her and that she did not need money. She said that her purpose in stopping him was to convey a warning, but Greene did not know sufficient German to comprehend what she was warning him against.

A few days later, the incident having slipped his mind, he received a telephone call at his office from a Mr. Pope who said he was in a Home Office aliens department and was interested to hear of a report that Greene had made to Sir Samuel Hoare concerning refugee conditions in Germany. He himself had been instructed to investigate further. This surprised Greene, as he had been stopped short by Hoare, who had told him, 'we have in our sources of information the evidence on which we can rely', effectively snubbing him and terminating the interview. Pope, however, wanted to meet Greene that night, as he claimed he was going up to Newcastle the next morning 'on a matter closely associated with the report'. Greene explained that he had an appointment in London that evening and it would be

11 p.m. before he was free. Pope said this was not too late for him, and as he lived at Mill Hill he pointed out that Greene would pass very close to his home on the way back to Berkhamsted.

Greene agreed to meet Pope at Burnt Oak underground station at 11.30 that night. When Greene arrived, he was met by a lady who introduced herself as Mrs. Pope, claiming her husband was delayed and inviting him to their house to wait for him. Reluctantly Greene agreed, for already his suspicions had been aroused. 'The lady was charming – too charming and very much made-up.' But on arriving at the house, Greene was temporarily relieved to find the door opened by a maid who later offered him sandwiches and a drink. 'Mrs. Pope' sat with him until 12.30 when she made a telephone call to her husband, returning to say it would be another hour before he came home. Greene said he could not wait and would make another appointment, when she suddenly 'turned all winsome, invited me to have some fun with her and even to get her into bed. I managed to shake her off, got my coat and went out to the car.'

Having escaped the grand seduction scene, Greene discovered to his dismay that two of his tyres had been let down. 'On going back to the house I could see the lady reflected in the mirror above the fireplace and, from her expression, I could see that she knew I would be back.' Greene asked the woman if he could phone the A.A., but as her charms had been rejected, she disdainfully refused to give him the number of the house they were in – a problem remedied by Greene going outside to look for himself. Once he had phoned the A.A. he sat down but 'kept my overcoat on'. Meanwhile, the lady vanished.

A little later, Greene heard a scuffle outside the front door of the house. Then it was flung open and two men accompanied by a police constable arrived. 'The first man came up to me asking what the hell was going on in his house and who I was. I said I was waiting for Mr. Pope with whom I had an appointment.' The man went on to ask who the hell Mr. Pope was. While the fracas continued, the police constable disappeared and Greene heard the noise of a vehicle outside, which he assumed to be the A.A. car. But when he looked out of the window he saw a private car driving away with the 'too charming' lady with whom Greene had spent such an eventful evening. Eventually Greene left, embarrassed but unhampered. He realized he had been the victim of a frame-up but could not understand why.

The reason, had he known it, was an attempt to undermine his position, but the two manufactured incidents aimed at discrediting Greene never came to anything because of the victim's lack of participation. He was, in fact, extremely attracted to women, a penchant Knight had very much relied on when he arranged these two incidents. Nevertheless they failed, and Knight was led to try a third gambit, this time introducing Kurtz. This attempt had very serious repercussions for all concerned. Greene emerged a broken man and Knight did considerable damage to his standing and future career. His moral justification for providing false evidence against Greene was, no doubt, that in Knight's view he was a Nazi-lover anyway and had to be interned for reasons of national security. If the evidence was lacking, then it was in the interests of national security to invent it.

When Greene was eventually interned in May 1940 no reason was given for his arrest. Over a year later, in response to the vigorous campaign of the Greene family and their lawyer, Oswald Hickson, the Home Office did in fact list the reasons for his detention:

Home Office
Advisory Committee
(Defence Regulations 18B)
6 Burlington Gardens
W.1.

10th June, 1941

REASONS FOR ORDER UNDER DEFENCE REGULATION 18B IN THE CASE OF BENJAMIN GREENE.

The order under Defence Regulation 18B was made against you, Benjamin GREENE, because the Secretary of State had reasonable cause to believe that you were a person of hostile associations and that by reason thereof it was necessary to exercise control over you.

Particulars

(1) You were born of a German mother, and your sister has remained in Germany since the outbreak of war, being either married or engaged to a German official, who is, or has been, working for the Germans.

(2) You have visited Germany on a number of occasions, and prior to the outbreak of war were in association or communication with German officials, including Beinemann, Hoffman and Bohle.

(3) You were, subsequent to the outbreak of war, communicating, and/or attempting to communicate with persons in Germany whom you knew, or suspected, to be in association with persons concerned in the government of Germany; and you counselled, assisted, and advised others as to the best means of sending messages into Germany by illicit channels.

(4) You were, subsequent to the outbreak of war, desirous of the establishment of a National Socialist regime in Great Britain with German co-operation if necessary, and endeavoured to make known your sentiments in this regard to those in control of the German Government.

(5) You freely associated with persons of German nationality whom you had reasons to believe were agents of the German Government and offered to assist them by every means in your power to avoid detention by the authorities in Great Britain, and to continue their work on behalf of Germany.

(6) As one of those concerned in the management and control of the British People's Party and the British Council for Christian Settlement in Europe you endeavoured in speeches and writings to persuade your

149

auditors and readers that the war was being waged solely for the benefit of financial interests, and could, and should, be brought to an end by a negotiated peace; that British policy, up to and after the outbreak of war, had been a policy of bluff and treachery; and that Hitler was justified in his invasion of Poland.

(7) You assisted John Beckett, alias John Stone, in the publication of pro-German propaganda in a periodical named "The Headline News Letter".

(8) There is reasonable cause to believe that, unless restrained, you desired and intended to continue the actions aforesaid, and actions of a like nature.

Greene's rebuttal of these charges was both positive and convincing. In relation to the first point Greene could not see why his mother's nationality could be termed 'hostile association', particularly as she had left Germany with her parents when she was three years old, and later married his father and lived in Brazil and England ever since. Her contact with Germany had been confined to her relatives. As to his sister, Barbara, he admitted that she lived in Germany but had little idea of her activities, relationships or occupation. He was not in correspondence with her at all.

With regard to the second point, Greene admitted visiting Germany in 1935 with Victor Botke, formerly a Reuters correspondent there, immediately after the Saar plebiscite, when he was Deputy Returning Officer. He went again in 1936 to hand over papers, again concerned with the plebiscite. There he was asked by the Society of Friends to look into stories of atrocities that had been reported in the English press. He did this and suggested that a group of Labour Party members should visit the area, an idea that was rejected. In the same year, he returned to Berlin to see the Olympic Games and in November 1938 returned again, once more on behalf of the Society of Friends, to enquire into the anti-Jewish riots and the conditions they spawned. He then tried to create a relief scheme for Jews whose lives had been made unbearable. The German Government, the Red Cross, the Quakers, as well as Protestants and Catholics, were all prepared to co-operate in looking at various means of getting Jews out of the country and, during negotiations, Greene had called to see Harry Bohle, who was prepared to act as an intermediary between Greene and the German Government.

But when Bohle heard of Greene's purpose he would have nothing whatever to do with it. Greene explained that he had done relief work in Germany in 1920 and that in Quaker relief work no account was taken of race, religion or politics. In Austria he had given relief to both Nazis and Communists at the same time. He then went on to outline the campaign he had run in England against the Versailles Treaty, the reparations muddle, and the weakness of the League of Nations in considering treaty revision.

Greene further explained that he had shown goodwill to Germany consistently throughout the last twenty years and he politely 'expressed my regret that they should not allow me even an approach to somebody in authority to discuss the question of Jewish relief'.

Bohle saw the force of Greene's argument and took him to the Ministry of Propaganda, where he saw some officials who were dealing with Jewish affairs. He was told that his propositions would be considered and their decisions later conveyed to him. It was provisionally agreed that he should return to Germany in January to draw up details of the relief scheme.

On his way back to England Greene called at Heidelberg, Frankfurt and Mainz where he found considerable Jewish enthusiasm for the scheme, at least until an official emigration policy could be devised.

Greene remained in contact with Bohle, who later told him that the scheme had been accepted in principle by the Ministry of Propaganda and confirmed his return trip in January or February. But in England difficulties had arisen, for there was dissension among Quaker groups as to the wisdom of the scheme and Greene was eventually told that it had been dropped. Therefore, his journey to Germany in January did not take place, but he continued to keep in touch with the German authorities in case the relief scheme should be revived or any alternative methods of helping refugees might be suggested by either Germany or England. 'As a Quaker the sincerity of my desires for peace should not be misunderstood and naturally this was a matter that came up in our correspondence.'

There was no possible doubt that Greene was acting entirely in a spirit of the greatest humanity and all evidence confirms this. It is a tragedy that there were not more like him to help alleviate the desperate plight of the Jews by actively assisting them as well as publicizing their situation.

With regard to Beinemann, Greene claimed he had known him only at a joint camp held in England with Berkhamsted School. He had never met Hoffman and had only received a publication called *News from Germany* indirectly from him.

Reasons three, four and five all referred to Greene's connections with Harald Kurtz and another of Knight's agents, Friedl Gaertner, the Austrian double agent who also worked for the German Secret Service and whose M.I.5 code name was Gelatine. Gaertner was the girl-friend of Dusko Popov (code name Tricycle), another double agent who was high up in the organization of the Abwehr (the German intelligence service) and who had recruited her for Knight. Later, Bill Younger was to fall in love with her, but the affair came to nothing. Her cover, as Wheatley's research assistant, was working well and for many months she supplied him with details of the backgrounds of the Nazi leaders, which Wheatley used as invaluable material for his Gregory Sallust spy stories.

Had Wheatley not been employing her, Gaertner would also have been interned unless some respectable citizen vouched for her. In her other capacity – controlled by Knight – Friedl Gaertner mainly worked in café society and several times she was picked up by the police as a tart. Joan Miller, secretly furious at being a dog's-body when she would have preferred to lead as exciting a life as Gaertner, was often sent by Knight to bail Gaertner out of Bow Street.

The third part of Knight's campaign to discredit Greene came when a letter from Harald Kurtz arrived through Greene's letter-box:

> 147 Ebury Street
> S.W.1
> Sloane 2558
> 12th March, 1940

Dear Sir

I owe your address to my friend Ilse von Binzer who as you know has left this country in August. She said very kindly at the time that I could get in touch with you if I wanted advice and I would have done so much earlier if I had not been interned since. Fortunately, however, I have just been released, and I am now more keen than ever to meet you if you can possibly spare the time. I do hope that Ilse has mentioned my name to you at the time.

I feel I must apologise for intruding like this, and I wish I would have met you earlier. You are not quite a stranger to me because about a year ago I applauded you when you had a little public argument with Dr. E. Ludwig at the Central Hall, Westminster.

> Yours very truly
> Harald Kurtz

Greene had known Fraulein von Binzer as the Secretary of Dr. Rosel at the Anglo-German Information Bureau, where he had often called for information sheets and, on one occasion, for the official versions of Hitler's speeches. Greene assumed Kurtz was just another refugee needing help, so he willingly went to his aid, little realizing that Kurtz was the trap Knight had set for him. He therefore called on him and was a little surprised that Kurtz had managed to obtain his release so easily by what appeared to be his own endeavours. Clearly, he was in dire financial straits, but Greene only enquired after Fraulein von Binzer and on this occasion, being suspicious, left Kurtz without making any other appointment or helping him in any way.

Disappointed, Kurtz reported back to Knight that Greene

was not co-operating. Knight told Kurtz to push him harder. He did so by phoning Greene's secretary stating that he wanted to speak to him on a matter of the greatest urgency. Once again, Greene did not respond and Kurtz rang continuously, reporting regularly back to Knight.

Knight's method of administering his agents and informers was to meet them in a variety of different locations, all of which were almost unnecessarily clandestine. The foyers of cheap hotels, railway station buffets, parks, museums, all were considered suitable venues for the mysterious Captain King to meet his subordinates – as Buchan would have it – 'meeting with odd people in odd places'. Kurtz, unlike many other agents, also lived in Dolphin Square and was sometimes allowed to see Knight in the office too. There or elsewhere he would receive precise instructions, two or three times a week, as to how he should proceed in the slow, but to Knight fascinating, job of ensnaring Greene. No doubt it reminded him of fishing, or poaching, on Exmoor.

Finally, Knight instructed Kurtz to write this letter:

> 147 Ebury Street
> London. S.W.1
> Sloane 2558

Dear Mr. Greene,   10.4.1940

I have been trying to ring you up at Berkhamsted but was never able to catch you in. Meanwhile I have met your sister Katherine and we had a frank and interesting talk.

I very much want to see you again, if you can possibly spare the time. I wonder if you could manage to have dinner here with me any evening next week which you would care to suggest. Or are you free this coming Sunday? Do forgive me for pestering you like this but you may understand that after the meeting at the Kings Hall and my talk with your sister, I am very keen to keep in touch with you.

> Yours very sincerely
> Harald Kurtz.

Eventually Greene's secretary, feeling persecuted, told the ever persistent Kurtz that her boss would meet him next time he was in London. Thus committed, Greene phoned Kurtz and was invited to tea at Ebury Street.

Over tea-cups, Greene discovered that Kurtz was not in difficulties himself, but that he had a friend, a refugee from Vienna, who was in great difficulties, and he felt that Greene was the most likely person to be able to help her. Kurtz continued to pile on the pressure and eventually the kindly Greene decided to make an appointment with her over supper. But despite this decision, he was still suspicious about Kurtz and later wrote in his defence paper: 'I was more than ever bewildered as to the kind of German Kurtz was. My experience with refugees had made it possible for me to classify the general run and Kurtz fitted no classification that I had come across. I finally thought he might either be a Communist with Nazi sympathies or more likely a Jew with Nazi sympathies.'

Over supper, Greene was given to understand that Fraulein Gaertner's fiancé was still in Austria and she was desperate to communicate with him there. She claimed that her fiancé held a high position and it would therefore be dangerous for him to be discovered communicating with a refugee. On this basis ordinary postal methods were impossible. 'It was suggested that as I was in touch with refugees I might know of ways whereby such letters could be sent.' But Greene knew of no method of avoiding either the German or the British censorship and said so most emphatically. Gaertner then suggested that Greene might know a Reuter correspondent returning to Switzerland who could take a message. But this request was strange because, although this ruse might well avoid the British censor, it would hardly evade the German one, and Gaertner must surely have realized this fundamental point.

Greene left Kurtz and Gaertner in an uneasy frame of mind, wondering what their real motives could be. There were so many inconsistencies in their conversation, and he was sure they were more anxious to avoid the British censor than the German one. As a magistrate, Greene felt that it was his duty to report it to the authorities. He therefore rang Scotland Yard and gave them the details. As a result he was asked what the message was that Gaertner and Kurtz were so anxious to despatch. But, of course, Greene had no idea. He was then told to keep the matter strictly to himself, find the content of the message, and pass it on to Scotland Yard who would afterwards be in touch with him. But the ever-liberal Greene decided against further action as he did not want to incriminate even suspect refugees and he heard no more from Scotland Yard.

Greene made no attempt to contact Kurtz and Gaertner again but was surprised to bump into them when deputizing for the Duke of Bedford at a meeting in the Holborn Hall where he spoke on the reform of the unemployment insurance scheme after the war. Knight had briefed Kurtz and Gaertner to try Greene again. After the meeting, Greene invited the dubious pair to supper, anxious only to discover the content of their message. But others joined them for the meal and no opportunity presented itself for cross-examination. Greene then invited Kurtz and Gaertner to Berkhamsted. He later cancelled the invitation 'as I am not out to act as a host to people I had reported to the police.' This vacillating approach, although frustrating to Knight and Kurtz, did at least make Greene look suspicious and Knight was able to close in.

On 23 May 1940 Greene was in Leicestershire, when his secretary told him that Scotland Yard wished to see him. Assuming he was wanted as a witness against Kurtz among the general arrests that were now taking place, Greene phoned the police and was asked to come to London that night. He complied and, on arrival, was arrested under Regulation 18B. Knight had decided that there was no further advantage to be gained by playing a waiting game.

In answer to point four of the charges against him, Greene stated that 'If the words National Socialist mean Nazi, then it is completely untrue that in Spring 1940 or at any other time I was desirous of setting up a Nationalist Socialist regime in this country.' He went on to state that the German authorities with whom he had contact were perfectly well aware that he was a socialist and that he regarded the British constitution as an inherent part of British life. He also stated that 'I would oppose Fascism as strongly as I have opposed Communism.' Greene added: 'If this sudden desire of mine to set up a Nazi state in Great Britain is based upon a statement made by Kurtz, then I must point out, in fairness to him, that I may have expressed admiration for certain aspects of the Nazi system in my endeavour to extract from him exactly where he, a German refugee, just released from detention, stood.'

As to his free association with persons of German nationality, Greene stated that he had had no reason to believe that Kurtz and Gaertner were agents of the German Government, nor had he attempted to shield them from the British authorities. On the contrary, he had reported Kurtz to Scotland Yard. Naturally, Knight did not reveal to Scotland Yard that Kurtz and Gaertner were M.I.5 agents, but he did persuade them to 'lose' the record they had kept of Greene's original telephone conversation about Kurtz.

In reply to point six of the 'Reasons for Order Under Defence Regulation 18B', Greene stated that he was certainly associated with the Duke of Bedford in starting the British People's Party in 1939, since he (Greene) had left the Labour Party. He claimed that his association was an 'endeavour to give expression to perfectly legitimate policies mainly concerned with the immediate issues of peace and war'. Greene felt the Labour Party had abandoned its peace policy and that the B.P.P. offered a means of expressing the desire for peace that existed distinct and separate from the National Socialist and Fascist bodies. Greene had formally severed all connections with the B.P.P. on 1 November 1939.

He believed that the British Council for Christian Settlement in Europe was a perfectly legitimate attempt to keep a body of non-party opinion alive to the danger of the new Versailles settlement and, at the same time, it expressed a strong desire for a negotiated peace. Greene denied that he had ever said war was being waged for the benefit of financial interests or that British policy up to the outbreak of war was a policy of bluff and treachery. With regard to Poland, he stated that his views had always been that Britain had made a major mistake of policy in guaranteeing Poland in 1939, when a previous attempt to give such a guarantee had been rejected at the polls and in Parliament in 1923.

With regard to point seven, Greene flatly denied that he had anything at all to do with Beckett and his 'Headline News Letter'.

Finally, Greene stated that 'there is nothing whatever to show that I desired or intended to pursue the actions complained of or actions of a like nature.'

On the night of 23 May, Ben Greene's wife, Leslie, phoned her brother-in-law Edward to say that her husband had been detained at Brixton Prison under the 18B regulation, though no charges had been made. Edward hurried to Brixton, finding it besieged by the hysterical families of those who had just been interned. Eventually he saw his brother, who was very shocked and, at that stage, had absolutely no idea why he had been detained and had received no explanation.

Finding his family lawyers of no help, Edward went to see Oswald Hickson, who was also representing the Mosleys. He told him that his brother had 'before the outbreak of war and subsequently, made, with the advantage of hindsight, some rather foolish statements, publicly and privately'.[7] In other words, Ben Greene, unlike many others, had had the courage to say what he believed in, however badly it was received or unfortunate his timing. Hickson wrote to the Home Office demanding the reasons for Greene's detention and eventually received a letter of explanation. Hickson then wrote to the Public Prosecutor demanding an immediate trial, but he refused, which made Hickson suspicious.

Knight had Edward's flat searched to see if he, too, was a security risk, but he found nothing of consequence. Then, while Hickson was trying to find out who was responsible for writing the report on Ben Greene, Edward had a visitor at his office. It

---

[7] Taken from an unpublished transcript given to me by Edward Greene.

was Harald Kurtz, sent by Knight to see if he could now trap Edward Greene.

Kurtz, to whom Edward took an instant dislike, said that he was sorry to hear that Ben had been interned and told Edward he knew him, recalling that he had also met Edward before. Edward replied politely enough, racking his brains to remember where he had met Kurtz. As Edward thought, he asked Kurtz what he was doing with himself. He replied, 'Oh, nothing very much, I have just been released from detention myself, from the Isle of Man.' When Edward asked him what the conditions had been like he said, 'Pretty awful, but the worst feature of all was that I had to mix with Jews.' But Edward could see that Kurtz was a Jew himself, so this made him thoroughly suspicious. After Kurtz left, Edward rang Hickson, who said, 'You be careful; they are after you.'

A few days later, Kurtz phoned Edward and said he wanted to see him again. Edward replied that he could see no purpose in any meeting at all, but Kurtz persisted, saying he was shortly going to Brazil and wanted Edward's advice about the country. Surprised, Edward asked Kurtz if he had a visa and he replied in the affirmative. Edward Greene then asked him to come to his office. Directly Kurtz had hung up, Edward dialled the Brazilian Consul whom he knew well, and asked him if he had issued a visa to Harald Kurtz. He said he had not.

Later that afternoon Kurtz duly arrived in Edward's office, claiming he wanted to start a new life in Brazil, but unfortunately did not know anybody out there. Edward replied that Kurtz, as a German national, could hardly expect letters of introduction to Edward's friends and Kurtz, reacting quickly, said he quite understood that he could not be introduced to English people but how about other nationalities? When Edward suggested that perhaps he meant Germans, Kurtz smiled and said, 'That would be very helpful.' Edward then asked him what would happen if he *did* write the letters and they were found on Kurtz? 'Oh, you can be absolutely sure that would never happen,' he replied. Eventually, Edward said, 'Thank you, Mr. Kurtz, I don't believe you are going to Brazil, but anyway, good-day,' and showed an unwilling Kurtz out of his office. Edward then phoned Hickson who said that if Edward had given him the letters he would have been in jail 'within five minutes'. Hickson went on to say that Greene had been the potential victim of a trick.

Later the Home Office told Hickson that the charges against Ben Greene had been made in a report written by Harald Kurtz. Hickson asked Edward to find Kurtz and bring him to Hickson's office. This was easier said than done, for Edward had absolutely no idea where Kurtz might be. He was in fact working for the department of the B.B.C. that was broadcasting propaganda to Germany, and, ironically, his immediate boss was Hugh Carleton Greene, Edward's cousin. Eventually Edward employed a detective agency and this agency discovered that Kurtz had a connection with Dolphin Square.

Dorothy Hunt, the inquiry agent involved, traced Kurtz but did not connect him with Knight, who was secreted behind the name of Coplestone. In her report, Hunt pin-pointed the anonymity of the flats:

> It is apparently possible to live on the estate without being known to the management as the subject is unknown by either name (Kurtz or Courts) to the letting office on the premises, the reception bureau staff, or to the private telephone exchange. It was pointed out that individuals are known by name only when they are direct tenants to the Dolphin Square Estate Company, and that persons in the position of sub-tenants usually pay through the actual leaseholder of the flat and thus frequently remain anonymous to the company.

She eventually ran Kurtz to earth via the porters in each block, finally establishing that he was living at Flat 10, Collingwood House, in Dolphin Square.

But there still seemed no way for Edward Greene to lure Kurtz into the Hickson net. Then, fortuitously, he met him outside the Café Royal in October 1941. Craftily, Edward greeted him as a friend and suggested that they should have lunch the next day at Simpsons in the Strand. Kurtz agreed and Edward phoned Hickson to tell him of the meeting. Together they plotted to trap Kurtz by inviting him round to the office after lunch. Careful not to bring up Ben's name at lunch, Edward left it to Kurtz to take the initiative. Over coffee, Kurtz asked about the case and Edward told him that the family were very puzzled by the whole affair and had come to the conclusion that there must have been a misunderstanding at the Home Office connected with Ben's Jewish relief work in Germany.

Then Edward told Kurtz that he might be of help. 'If you can spare me a few moments,' he said, 'I'll see if Hickson is in his office and perhaps you would care to come round with me.' After some hesitation, Kurtz agreed. The dramatic denouement swiftly followed. In the lawyer's office, Hickson, flanked by his secretary and clerk, stood up and said, 'Mr. Harald Kurtz, my name is Oswald Hickson, Solicitor. I am acting on behalf of Ben Greene, who is detained under Defence Regulation 18B, and I want now to read you the charges under which he has been detained.' Edward noticed that Kurtz immediately began to sweat.

After Hickson had read out the charges he told them that they had been based on a report made by one Harald Kurtz. He asked Kurtz if that was his identity, upon which Kurtz, growing excited, jumped to his feet and exclaimed, 'This is a trap; I refuse to say anything more.' But eventually Kurtz admitted he had lied about Greene and agreed to sign a statement admitting this. It was a swift climb-down and Hickson and Edward Greene were very elated at turning the tables on Kurtz.

Two months later, after Hickson and Edward had appeared before a committee of enquiry, Ben Greene was released. Within a few days the Home Office wrote, saying: 'In respect of the detention and the reasons for this detention, the charge may be considered withdrawn.'

Knight was furious with Kurtz and gave him a severe dressing-down for his naivety and clumsiness. In his turn Knight had to answer to Harker and Liddell who could not understand how such an experienced M.I.5 case officer could have employed such an incompetent agent. First Bill Allen, now Harald Kurtz. Liddell in particular began to look askance at Knight, wondering if he had had his day.

In March 1941, while still in Brixton, Ben Greene had applied to the King's Bench Division for a writ of habeas corpus but the Home Secretary, Sir John Anderson, refused it, stating that 'I carefully studied the reports and considered the information and I came to the conclusion that there was clear cause to believe, and I did in fact believe, that Benjamin Greene was a person of hostile associations and that by reason thereof it was necessary to exercise control over him.[8] So habeas corpus was refused and although the request was taken to the House of Lords, they were bound by the terms of Regulation 18B. Without Kurtz's statement it is unlikely that Greene would have been released.

Two days before Greene's release, on 22 January 1942, the Home Secretary, Herbert Morrison, was asked whether 'proceedings would be taken against the person or persons upon whose evidence Mr. Ben Greene was detained under Regulation 18B?'

He replied: 'Mr. Greene was not detained on the evidence of a single person. There was undisputed information derived from various sources that he had hostile associations; and these associations were of such a character that it was necessary to exercise some control over him. Even at this date his release from detention has been made subject to conditions imposed for this purpose. The information, however, included certain allegations which rested largely on information given by a single person. After considering the recent report by the Advisory Committee I came to the conclusion that these particular allegations should be regarded as withdrawn and I have caused Mr. Greene to be informed accordingly. The fact that certain information may be regarded as unsubstantiated does not indicate that the informant has committed a criminal offence for which proceedings can be taken.' But in fact, the only real

[8] Public Record Office.

evidence against Ben Greene was the fabrications in Kurtz's report.

Greene was in very bad shape when he was released; twenty months in prison had undermined his health and mental state. Edward took an ambulance to Brixton Prison and, in it, Ben Greene was transferred to St. Mary's Hospital, Paddington. He suffered from a persecution complex for the rest of his life.

The *New Statesman and Nation* saw the unfairness of Ben Greene's situation and, on 24 January 1942, wrote:

> Mr. Ben Greene . . . was detained last May under 18B on a number of counts. These may be divided into two categories. The first were suspicions due to Mr. Greene's 'hostile associations'; that is, the Home Secretary felt that in view of Mr. Greene's political activities, connections, etc., he was better under detention at a period of acute national danger. Mr. Greene is now released because, as Mr. Morrison explains, adequate precautions can be taken without Mr. Greene's detention. Somewhat curiously, Sir John Anderson, who originally detained Mr. Greene, appears to have given an affidavit asserting that in the Home Secretary's opinion, Mr. Greene was also guilty of a number of very serious criminal offences, which amount in fact to accusations of Fifth Columnism and treason. These allegations, which became public in the course of legal proceedings in the House of Lords, are now, in the words of Mr. Morrison's letter, 'to be regarded as withdrawn'. No one, least of all Mr. Greene, who has come out of Brixton suffering from six foot seven inches of rheumatism, can be satisfied with this apology. Some further restitution would appear to be necessary now that it is officially admitted that these charges were unfounded. The House of Commons was highly critical of Mr. Morrison on the 18B issue which arose in Mr. Gibbs' article in the *Economist* before Christmas. It is likely to take the view that the Home Secretary's affidavit making allegations apparently on insufficient and highly suspect evidence

justifies Lord Atkins' opinion that the Home Secretary ought not to be the sole judge of evidence on which a man can be deprived of his reputation and his liberty.

But there was no restitution for Ben Greene for having been wrongly accused on evidence supplied by M.I.5, as the Official Secrets Act made it impossible to publish the truth. On 29 January 1942, at the House of Commons, Morrison was still under pressure to give reasons for Greene's detention. When asked whether he would reveal the name of the single person on whose evidence Ben Greene was detained under Regulation 18B, Morrison insisted that Greene was not detained on the evidence of a single person at all. He also added that it would be contrary to the public interest to publish the names of 'persons who give confidential information'. Later, he insisted: 'The evidence he gave was not the sole evidence on which Mr. Greene was detained by an Order made by my predecessor. I have read the papers and I should not regard his [Kurtz's] evidence as necessarily being the evidence which solely determined the detention.'[9]

Ben Greene brought an action against the Home Secretary for false imprisonment, but this failed because the court was not concerned with the truth or falsity of the charges, but only with the subjective 'reasonable cause' in the mind of the Home Secretary. The action also failed because the Home Secretary claimed privilege from disclosure of all official documents which were 'essential evidence for the plaintiff's case'. During the course of this case, the detective agency employed by the Greene family to observe Kurtz discovered a direct connection between him and Knight. This should have been a piece of invaluable evidence for the Greenes but, because they had no idea that Knight was connected with M.I.5, it is only with the publication of this book that the record can be set straight.

The inquiry agent, this time a Mr. William Philp, reported that:

[9] Hansard.

Re Kurtz

As instructed I made enquiries on Thursday, the 23rd inst., with the object of tracing and serving Mr. Harold Kurtz [*sic*].

The portress informed me that, so far as she knew, Mr. Harold Kurtz never occupied a flat in Collingwood House, but he was in the habit of visiting people there by the name of Knight, who were the tenants occupying 010 prior to the present tenants. Occasionally Mr. Kurtz slept in the flat. When the Knights left for an unknown destination, Mr. Kurtz was supposed to have taken a flat at 612 Hood House, but to her definite knowledge he had not done so, and she had seen nothing of him now for some months.

But Philp was unable to trace Kurtz, although eventually the Greene family managed to have him named in the House of Lords. As a result Kurtz's cover was blown and Knight, who had tried so hard to discredit Ben Greene, was himself discredited. Not only was his credibility seriously undermined but, because of this, less attention was paid to his fears about Soviet infiltration of M.I.5 than was warranted.

But Knight had left Ben Greene in a far worse position. On the basis of 'no smoke without fire' many people in Berkhamsted regarded him as a traitor and, although his factory workforce remained loyal, he was not reinstated as a magistrate, a position from which he had been removed when he was interned.

Writing in a pamphlet regarding this dismissal, Greene stated: 'At a ruinous cost I have now tried every legal method to secure my vindication, and I have got nowhere. My removal from the Bench I must accept as final. What I cannot accept as final is the principle that we have an imprisonment without trial legally recognised in England.'

Joan Wooton, his personal secretary for many years, told me: 'Ben always suffered from the effects of 18B and it pursued him until the end of his life. ... He was an isolationist, a

165

perfectionist, an idealist. Ben was also a bad judge of character and this in itself had led him into dangerous company.' But Joan Wooton knows there was no question of Ben Greene being a traitor. He was simply a humanitarian who tried to help refugees and was shattered by his internment.

Somewhat ironically, Greene had come to know Captain Ramsay well in prison and it was Ramsay who was later responsible for recommending Greene's young son, Paul, for Eton, despite the fact that his name had not been put down at birth. In the late forties, Ramsay left his wife Ismay to live with a girl-friend in London, and Ben Greene gave him a room in his house in Berkhamsted so that the two lovers could be together. Leslie von Goetz, one of Ben Greene's daughters, remembers that Ramsay, Pitt-Rivers, Barry Domvile and one or two other non-Mosleyite detainees had talked for many hours with Ben Greene in Brixton Prison. He was the only detainee with a left-wing background and there was a considerable exchange of views.

Ben Greene was a martyr to the Quaker cause and a victim of Knight's ruthless determination. He died in March 1978, still haunted by his prison experience. Knight had been convinced that Greene had behaved traitorously, but in using Kurtz as an *agent provocateur* he had erred seriously. Knight himself should have admitted as an English 'gentleman' that this just wasn't cricket, but instead, despite Greene's so-called acquittal, he continued to have him watched closely.

Further evidence of the dubious means Knight employed to maintain Greene's internment came to light some ten years after the war. He had just returned from his Scottish works to his Berkhamsted office when he was told there was someone waiting for him. He had apparently called several times before. When the man entered Greene's office he greeted him with the words, 'I hope you do not remember me', and went on to say that he had been one of the investigators in Greene's internment and that at one time he had interviewed him in Brixton Prison. He was now retired and to some extent free to speak.

Greene wrote in his unpublished manuscript: 'He wanted to apologise for the unfair aspersions he cast upon me at the interview in Brixton. Some of his colleagues had become very uneasy at the part they were required to play in the case of some of the detentions and he was particularly uneasy over the part he had played in mine.' Greene's visitor went on to explain that the 'letter on which I was cross examined in my action for false imprisonment was ... forged. The process was a very simple one. On my arrest my place of work and residence was searched and among the papers removed would be blank letter heading. With these letters could be typed of the most incriminating sentiments. They would then be stamped with a rubber copy of my signature. These would then be photocopied. But where on the original it would be clear that the signature was rubber stamped, on the copy this would not be obvious.' When the Treasury solicitors asked for the originals Greene claimed it was explained to them that they had been intercepted before the war. The originals had been sent on and so were not available. Several of these letters 'had been prepared when it was apparent that the bottom of the case against me had fallen through'. Greene stated that this became certain when his solicitors had finally traced Kurtz and were able to serve a subpoena on him. The fact that he had been given two different reasons for his detention was not due to a mistake but was a deliberate act by someone in the Home Office by whom the Advisory Committee had been misled.

Greene's visitor then told him that just before the accusations against him were formally withdrawn, instructions (presumably from M.I.5) had been issued to 'see what skeletons could be unearthed in my cupboard. ... Before leaving he wished me well and he concluded by saying that I must have aroused a very great degree of enmity in some influential circles.'

Although the case broke both Knight and Greene in different ways, even more lasting damage was done to Great Britain's security when, as a result of his loss of credibility, successive Directors-General of M.I.5 did not take Knight seriously enough, and did not heed his valid warnings against Communist infiltration. But Knight only had himself to blame. He had begun to invent the rules of the game.

CHAPTER NINE

KNIGHT AS PROPHET: 1940–1943

KNIGHT had been very alert to the dangers of Communist infiltration ever since the discovery of the Woolwich Arsenal spy ring, and had increasingly suspected Communist infiltration inside M.I.5 itself. However, because of his mishandling of the Ben Greene affair his warnings were ignored. As a result such major figures as Burgess, Maclean, Philby and Blunt were able to spy for Russia completely unsuspected. It was not until the Driberg affair that Knight had any concrete evidence to back up his suspicions.

Born in 1905, Tom Driberg was five years younger than Knight and a self-confessed homosexual. He had joined the Brighton branch of the Communist Party while still at Lancing College in Sussex and had remained a member throughout his years at Oxford and as a journalist on the *Daily Express*, despite the apparent contradictions between his private convictions and the nature of his work. Michael Foot wrote in his postscript to Driberg's autobiography *Ruling Passions*:[1] 'I first met Tom in the late 1930s, in his Beaverbrook-Stalinite heyday, and by that I mean when he combined his William Hickey column in the *Express* with the profession of the most Orthodox Communist-Party-line politics.'

In 1942 Driberg became Labour M.P. for Maldon in Essex. Like Knight, Driberg had had a very difficult childhood, and the

[1] (Jonathan Cape, 1977).

part of Philip Larkin's poem from his collection *High Windows*,[2] quoted in *Ruling Passions*, has relevance to the problems of both men.

> They fuck you up, your mum and dad.
> They may not mean to but they do.
> They fill you with the faults they had
> And add some extra, just for you.
>
> But they were fucked up in their turn
> By fools in old-style hats and coats,
> Who half the time were soppy-stern
> And half at one another's throats.

Driberg's father, former chief of police in India, died when he was fourteen and he remembered him only as a remote Edwardian figure in failing health. He loved his mother deeply but resented the Freudian interpretation of this. 'The term "very close" seems to me detestable,' he wrote, 'in its suffocating cosiness.' His childhood was very lonely and he became increasingly solitary as he grew into adolescence. His mother had been thirty-nine when he was born and he had two elder brothers, both in their early twenties by the time he was five. He therefore lacked childhood companions and, although he spent some holidays with a group of young cousins, he was never really at ease with them. Nevertheless, Driberg wrote: 'Much as I have sometimes regretted the mess my life has largely been – and some of this must be attributable to the circumstances of my childhood – it would not be reasonable to blame my parents for behaving according to the customs, obsolescent even then, of their age and class. It is I who was "born out of due time".'[3]

Driberg's ardent homosexuality began to develop during a miserable prep-school career and he started to make encounters in public lavatories when he was an adolescent. He also had a passion for churches – either high Anglican or Roman Catholic

[2] (Faber, 1974).
[3] *Ruling Passions*.

– where he discovered religion, loving the mysticism of the mass. At Lancing, having found the Labour Party lifeless, Driberg joined the Brighton branch of the Communist Party and was told to sell the *Daily Worker* in his Sussex home town of Crowborough. As Crowborough was essentially middle-class and full of retired colonels, his task was difficult. His membership of the C.P.G.B. continued while he was at Oxford and it was about this time that he met Aleister Crowley. They lunched at the Eiffel Tower restaurant in London, where Driberg remembered Crowley greeting him in a well-cut plus-four suit of green hand-woven tweed and saying in a high donnish voice: 'Pardon me while I invoke the Moon.' Driberg kept up a friendship with Crowley and indeed Crowley dubbed him his successor as World Teacher at one point, although Driberg discovered later that he had also offered the post to someone else. But the relationship was to be another bond with Knight at a later stage.

After Oxford Driberg continued his prolific sexual encounters usually with 'rough trade', young working-class men he picked up in London or anywhere else he could find them. For a while he lived on friends' loans in London and became involved with the literati – Edith Sitwell and her penny-bun tea-parties where he met T. S. Eliot and Aldous Huxley. Eventually, through the influence of the Sitwell brothers, he joined the *Daily Express*. Starting as a reporter, he was transferred to the 'Talk of London' gossip column, and when this was killed by Beaverbrook he became a reporter on the William Hickey column, which was originally designed to introduce a sharper note, still containing information about 'Names', but modelled on *Time*'s economical prose.

Driberg first came to Knight's attention when he began to write Hickey and he was recruited to infiltrate the circles of what Beaverbrook termed 'the Café Communists'. Beaverbrook not only tolerated Driberg's membership of the C.P.G.B. but also turned a blind eye to his promiscuity, largely because of his considerable skill as a journalist. In a satirical piece in the 'Londoner's Diary' of the *Evening Standard*, of 19 May 1938, partly written by Beaverbrook himself, great scorn was poured on the Café Communists:

> The Café Communists are one of the more recent products of our modern social life.
>
> They are the gentlemen, often middle-aged, who gather in fashionable restaurants, and, while they are eating the very fine food that is served in those restaurants and drinking the fine wines of France and Spain, they are declaring themselves to be of Left Wing faith.

Among these so-called Café Communists was the distinguished left-wing publisher Victor Gollancz, who while not actually a member of the C.P.G.B., was very sympathetic to their views and had, with John Strachey (for whom Olga Gray had worked), formed the Left Book Club in March 1936. Knight was very interested in the club, as it represented a specific attempt to unite Communists, Socialists and Liberals in Great Britain. This purpose was fronted by the wider ideal of opposing Fascism, but Knight had seen behind this from the beginning. During its first year the club had published Palme Dutt's *World Politics 1918–1936*, among a selection of other books that actually promoted Communism, and over the next eighteen months Gollancz and his Left Book Club had reached an amazing subscription figure of 50,000. A large number of public meetings were organized right up to the beginning of the war. Harry Pollitt, the General Secretary of the C.P.G.B., spoke at some of the meetings and Knight was particularly anxious to have all his actions carefully monitored.

Beaverbrook, writing in the same 'Londoner's Diary' column, allowed Driberg the 'right of reply'. In other words he wrote it and gave Driberg the passing courtesy of having it read over to him:

> Another is Tom Driberg, the columnist. When taxed with this incongruity between his views and his surroundings, Mr. Driberg reports that he does not see why he also

should be a victim of the malnutrition which is an endemic disease of capitalism; that clear thinking need not imply poor feeding; that since the most painful part of his job is to associate occasionally with the rich and powerful, he naturally, on such occasions, needs an anaesthetic; and that he has yet to discover a really 'fine' Spanish wine anyway.

With this in mind, Knight asked Driberg if he would report back to him on anything he discovered at the C.P.G.B. that would affect the security of the country and he promised to do so. But he was not asked to spy on any one person or to initiate an arrest, simply to observe and report back. Driberg was not a serious enough Party member to regard this behaviour as disloyal, and besides, he needed Knight's help to conceal his promiscuity which was increasing and might well have become too conspicuous for even Beaverbrook to whitewash. Driberg favoured a particular male brothel in Essex and Knight gave him a telephone number so that, if he ran into trouble there, he could phone for assistance. The kind of assistance that was open to him might have been financial, over-ruling an arrest or discouraging a potential blackmailer. So Driberg received protection while Knight received information.

Joan Miller alleges that Knight asked her several times if she would like to visit the brothel but she declined, claiming she found Knight's vicarious interest alarming. But whatever Knight's feelings were about Driberg's sex-life, he always enjoyed his company, for he was not only a brilliant journalist but also an entertaining and intelligent companion. Joan, embittered by her rejection, remembered that Knight had been infiltrating the C.P.G.B. for many years and, even after the Russians had joined the British side in the war, he considered it vital to maintain the infiltration. Knight had known Driberg well before Joan came on the scene and she now claims that Knight was 'in his own particular way, crazy about him'. But this is her own subjective view. Joan also privately considered Driberg unreliable as an agent.

But Driberg *did* have his uses, for he was friendly not only

with Harry Pollitt but also with Douglas Springhall, a promi-
nent office-holder in the Party who was later (1943) convicted
for spying for the Soviets. Unwittingly, however, Driberg
served the wider purpose of alerting Knight to the Soviet
infiltration of M.I.5.

It was Anthony Blunt who brought Driberg's work as an
M.I.5 agent to an abrupt end. Blunt was born in 1902 and spent
most of his childhood in Paris where his father was vicar of the
English church and also chaplain to the British Embassy. It was
a period when Blunt first began to fall in love with French
painting. An aesthete among hearties at Marlborough, he
continued his education in art with his older brother Wilfrid,
later art master at Eton and a writer. By 1926, Blunt was at
Trinity College, Cambridge, where he read modern languages,
took a First and, in 1932, became a Fellow of his college. While
at Cambridge, he was elected a member of the Apostles, the
exclusive club which spawned much Communist thought. He
was also a declared homosexual and a member of the group of
young Communists which included Burgess and Maclean.
Burgess convinced Blunt that the Marxist interpretation of
history was the only right path and recruited him as a
Communist agent. Originally Blunt had acted as a talent-spotter
for Burgess, but during the war he collected considerable
information for the Russians concerning internal defence,
security and foreign policy, in particular, the attitude of the
British Government to neutral countries.

By 1939 Blunt had joined the army as a second lieutenant and
applied for an intelligence posting. He was turned down because
an investigation into his background revealed Marxist associations at Cambridge. Amazingly, a year later, after having
served with the British Expeditionary Force, he was cleared to
joint M.I.5 when, as it turned out, he was at all times in contact
with his Russian case officer.

When Anthony Blunt was recruited by M.I.5, he became part
of F Branch, which was responsible for trying to identify
suspected fifth columnists. During the last few months of 1940
he was in charge of running the Watcher Service, which

kept certain suspected subversives under careful observation. Therefore, some of the surveillance of so-called pro-Nazi sympathizers was also in the hands of Blunt and, as a result, six of the 140 files in the Home Office series (released in November 1983) have been retained. These will eventually show the extent of M.I.5's concern over Moscow's involvement in fifth-column activities; at present they are still considered to be highly sensitive politically.

Blunt was later moved to become personal assistant to Guy Liddell, then Director of B Division (Counter-Espionage). After two months he was moved again, this time into B1(b) where he was responsible for checking the diplomatic pouches of neutral countries, a position in which he remained until 1944. He also represented M.I.5 at the weekly meetings of the Joint Intelligence Committee whose responsibility it was to assess information from numerous sources for Churchill and his chiefs of staff. He was therefore in an excellent position to pass invaluable information to the Russians.

Always alert to the possibility of Soviet infiltration, Knight acquired his first piece of irrefutable evidence when Driberg was unmasked. He submitted written reports to Knight and these were identified as reports from M8, though Driberg himself was not aware of his label. Blunt, although not a member of the Dolphin Square set, saw a copy of such a report in someone else's office in St. James's Street and at once noted that it referred to Communist knowledge of a secret British aeroplane. He showed the content of the report to his Soviet case officer who instructed him to discover the identity of M8. Because of B5(b)'s independence from the main body of M.I.5 this was extremely difficult to achieve, and six months elapsed before Blunt could make any progress. Then he saw another report from M8 which mentioned a book that Driberg had recently published, and Blunt was able to identify him at last.

In 1941, retribution from the C.P.G.B. was swift and clumsy. Driberg was on his way to a branch meeting with a print worker named Harry Kennedy, who was an old and trusted friend. When they stopped at a pub for a drink, Driberg found

Kennedy both silent and ill at ease. After some time he blurted out that he had been instructed to inform him that he had been expelled from the Party. Considerably shaken, Driberg angrily asked for the reason for his expulsion but Kennedy replied that he had no idea and was only a messenger.

Mortified, Driberg later went to see the most influential Party members he knew, among them Robin and Olive Page Arnot and David Springhall, posing the same question. But, in some embarrassment, they responded as negatively as Kennedy. They had no idea at all why he had been so summarily dismissed. Although Driberg kept up this public image of angry enquiry, he did, in fact, know exactly why he had been expelled, although this did not lessen his distress at the severing of the link. Nevertheless, it did do him the service of permitting him to stand for Parliament as a left-wing independent in 1942, for he was honestly able to state that he belonged to no party. Blunt, however, was furious, for the abrupt unsubtle expulsion might have undermined his own position, as it was obvious to anyone looking on that the denunciation could only have come from M.I.5 sources. But no one *was* looking, except Knight, and he was not listened to.

Obviously, Knight's loss of status prevented him from being taken seriously on this important task. A senior case officer in M.I.5 cannot afford to make mistakes, particularly in the light of inter-departmental jealousies. Some of Knight's more recent case-work had been shown up as either exceptionally inept and misguided, or, worse still, totally wrong, as in the Greene affair. Knight's department, with its enviable independence, was also a natural target for those in M.I.5 who were jealous not only of B5(b) but of Knight's personal link to Desmond Morton.

One of those who failed to listen and continuously blocked Knight was Roger Hollis. Chapman Pincher, in his sensational book *Their Trade is Teachery*,[4] claimed that Hollis himself was a Soviet agent, but there is little direct evidence for this, although, as this book goes to press, new accusations are being made

[4] (Sidgwick and Jackson, 1981.)

against him. Hollis joined M.I.5 in 1940 with the rank of Assistant Director, having spent some years in the Far East with British American Tobacco. He swiftly became the key figure responsible for monitoring Communist operations in the U.K. as well as the colonies, serving on Swinton's Communist Activities Committee, and it was to Hollis that Knight, just after Driberg's expulsion from the C.P.G.B. in 1941, sent a long report entitled 'The Comintern is not Dead'. It dealt with his conviction that there was considerable Soviet penetration in the British security services and called for an immediate investigation. But Hollis rejected the report, considering that Knight's long history of Communist Party surveillance had made him obsessive.

Furious at his rejection, Knight sent his report to Liddell, Director of B Division, who also turned it down. Eventually Knight went over Hollis and Liddell's heads to Desmond Morton. Morton gave it to Churchill to read but he showed little reaction. His enemy was Nazi Germany and he did not regard security service personnel having left-of-centre political views as particularly dangerous. Certainly Communists were not officially allowed to be members of M.I.5, but C.P.G.B. members like Driberg were used as agents for obvious reasons.

Determined not to be put off, Knight continued his surveillance of the C.P.G.B. at King Street, although by now they were very suspicious. He tapped their phones, opened their post and was partly responsible for arresting David Springhall in 1943. Springhall, a member of the C.P.G.B.'s central commitee since 1932, had been dismissed from the Royal Navy for causing dissension. He had fought in the Spanish Civil War against Franco, and, after the defeat of the Communists, returned to London to become the C.P.G.B.'s national organizer.

Springhall was kept under surveillance and, in 1942, was found to be trying to pump information out of Olive Sheehan, a Customs and Excise clerk working at the Air Ministry. Special Branch arrested her quietly and she received three months' imprisonment, after agreeing to give evidence against Springhall, a fact that was given no publicity at all. Sheehan told Knight that

Springhall had said to her that he was reliably informed the British Government was planning to prevent vital information from reaching Stalin. His informant turned out to be an S.O.E. agent named Captain Ormond Uren, who had earlier been dropped into Hungary and was now working in the S.O.E. headquarters in Baker Street. There he had access to top secret eastern European intelligence information, material that he passed on to Springhall. Following one of their meetings, Springhall was arrested by Special Branch. Uren was later court-martialled. They each received a sentence of seven years.

Meanwhile, Joan Miller had obtained information from a most unlikely source concerning Guy Burgess, who was then freelancing for M.I.5 while working for the B.B.C. At the time she had never heard of Burgess and a golden opportunity to help Knight and his anti-Communist campaign was missed. Meeting an elderly lady in St. Ermin's Hotel in Westminster (a favourite M.I.5 haunt), Joan was told that there was a man in the B.B.C. called Guy Burgess who was a Soviet agent. After a lengthy session with her informant, Joan wrote a brief report recommending further investigation, although she knew that it was unlikely to be followed up, as the elderly lady was notorious inside B5(b) for making accusations. Nevertheless, for years afterwards Joan was to remember the words: 'Now, my dear, whatever you do, make sure you do something about this man.'

Although his prophecies were dismissed at the time, Knight was later proved right: Guy Burgess and Donald Maclean fled to the Soviet Union in 1951; Kim Philby defected in 1964; Anthony Blunt confessed in 1965, although he was not publicly exposed until 1979; and Hollis, at his own request, was investigated in 1970 over allegations that he had been a Soviet mole during his period as Director-General of M.I.5 between 1956 and 1965. He was, on this occasion, cleared of all suspicion.

In 1964 Blunt admitted to his M.I.5 interrogators that he had been closely questioned at the time about the Driberg affair but that he had managed to avoid ultimate suspicion. This was a lucky escape. Either Pollitt had been briefed wrongly or he had acted with clumsy haste. Clearly he should have waited, letting time elapse, before expelling Driberg.

John Bingham, Knight's deputy, now reflects: 'Max didn't like Blunt – and he didn't want to work with him. He used to say that he wouldn't have "that bugger" round the section' (department). Perhaps this was his very acute intuition, but in fact it is more likely that he did not trust Blunt's sophisticated, elegant, aesthetic, homosexual ways.

Driberg's expulsion from the C.P.G.B. did not impair his relationship with Knight, and he remained an M.I.5 agent as well as a close personal friend. When he became an M.P. in 1942 he was able to pass on to Knight interesting information on the public and private lives of various Members of Parliament. Later, Pollitt apologized to Driberg for the manner of his expulsion, excusing himself on the grounds that he had been in receipt of wrong information. Pollitt went on to suggest that Driberg rejoin the C.P.G.B. secretly so that he could report back to them on parliamentary affairs, just as he was doing for Knight. Knight knew of Driberg's double-agenting, and was also aware that Driberg loved gossip and role-playing, so the value of his information to both sides was very erratic.

Knight was made very angry by the lack of interest shown by Churchill in his report about the Comintern. He was certain that he was right and that the danger was very great. On the other hand, he knew all too well that he was not being taken seriously any longer, even by Morton. He had risked too much and cut too many corners.

CHAPTER TEN

THE PUBLIC MAN: 1944–1968

WITH the end of the Second World War in Europe in May
1945, M.I.5 began to reduce its personnel. The divisions
remained the same, but the secrecy surrounding Knight's B5(b)
office at Dolphin Square and its autonomy were soon to come
under attack from M.I.5's new Director-General, Sir Percy
Sillitoe.

Sillitoe succeeded Petrie, now 66, on 30 April 1946, much
to the disappointment of Harker, Petrie's Deputy Director-
General, who was not considered to have the necessary powers
of leadership, and Guy Liddell (Director of B Division and
Knight's immediate boss) who, although an outstanding intelligence officer, was known to mix in homosexual circles.

Sillitoe became Director-General of M.I.5 on the same day that
Allan Nunn May, the atom spy, was charged at the Old Bailey.
The appointment of Sillitoe broke with M.I.5 tradition, for Kell
and Petrie had service backgrounds while Sillitoe came from the
police. In 1908 he had joined the British South African Police
Force, later transferring to the Northern Rhodesian Police and
serving in the German East African campaign during World
War I. When Sillitoe returned to England at the end of the war,
he became a highly successful police officer, creating Britain's
first forensic science department as Chief Constable of Sheffield
in 1929, and fighting gang-land crime as Chief Constable of
Glasgow. In April 1943, Sillitoe became Chief Constable of
Kent and, in 1946, Director-General of M.I.5.

The ramifications were wide, for M.I.5 officers were greatly affronted by control passing from the military to a mere policeman. Harker was given early retirement the following year and Liddell took his place as Deputy Director. The disappearance of Knight's confidant Harker left him in a vulnerable position, as did the removal of his other confidant, Desmond Morton, when Churchill was replaced by Attlee and his Labour government in 1945. Knight no longer had powerful friends to protect him and to maintain the secrecy that had for so long surrounded his department and his activities. Sillitoe himself particularly disliked the layers of secrecy he discovered in M.I.5 and wrote that during his first few weeks as Director-General he found it so 'extremely difficult to find out precisely what everyone was doing that I felt its popular reputation for excessive secrecy was in no way exaggerated.'[1] Sillitoe's appointment was largely due to Attlee, who was suspicious of the secrecy and blamed M.I.5 for the trouble about the Zinoviev letter which, in 1924, had brought about the fall of the Labour government. Certainly, Sillitoe aptly summed up Knight's department when he went on to state: 'The men whom I was attempting to direct were highly intelligent, but somehow introspective, each working, it seemed to me, in a rather withdrawn isolation, each concentrating on his own special problems.'

Derek Tangye, M.I.5 press officer during World War II, felt the same. 'There was so much secrecy within secrecy. My colleagues were charming and amiable, conscientious and erudite, but sometimes when I was talking to one of them a glazed expression would come over his face; and I would try to make up my mind whether he was hiding information from me or whether he felt at a disadvantage because I had shown I knew more than he did.'[2]

Sillitoe's view was that M.I.5 should not have so much power that it reached the level of a secret police department in a

---

[1] From an article entitled 'My Answer to Critics of M.I.5', by Sir Percy Sillitoe in the *Sunday Times*, 22 November 1953.
[2] *The Way to Minack* (Michael Joseph, 1968).

totalitarian state and he was extremely concerned that it might well head that way. Knight, however, openly condemned Sillitoe for his lack of professionalism, i.e. his campaign against excessive secrecy. Despite the Greene débâcle, Knight was as much in love with the clandestine as ever.

Joyce, whom Knight had failed to intern, had been caught and was executed at Wandsworth on 3 January 1946; Mosley had been released unrepentant but with severe phlebitis on 20 November 1943; while Greene had left Brixton in 1941. Anna Wolkoff remained in prison, serving her ten-year sentence; Kent was deported to the States in 1945; and Ramsay left Brixton in 1944. These big fish, and many minor but important catches, convinced Knight of his own continuing importance and – above all – potential. But Sillitoe saw him as a relic of the past. He ordered the closure of the Dolphin Square flats and Knight and his colleagues were forced to move into the new counter-subversion department, F3, with the *hoi polloi* at M.I.5's new building at Leconfield House in Curzon Street. Blenheim Palace had now been taken over once again by its owner, the Duke of Marlborough, and without excursions to the country or the permanent bolt-hole at Dolphin Square, Knight found himself both constricted and exposed.

To make matters worse, his private life had been in the doldrums since he and Joan had parted with such acrimony. He was lonely and in need of another female prop. Then, in 1944, Joan introduced him to a young woman she had met from the M.I.5 Registry at Blenheim. Her name was Susi Barnes and she had just ended a disastrous affair with an overseas agent, which had given her a terror of sexual intercourse.

'She was ideal for Max,' Joan said. 'She was safe.'

Susi was fifteen years younger than Knight and saw him as a courteous, kindly, father-figure who would be understanding about her sexual fears and make no demands on her. She came from bankrupt landowning stock in Kent, had been 'finished' in Austria and was twenty-nine when she and Knight met. They were married in 1944 and, ironically, went to live at the house in Camberley where Knight had resided in such style with Joan Miller. There Susi accustomed herself to Knight's menagerie which now included birds, frogs, toads and snakes which he kept in the house or the back garden. She also helped to care for a parrot which regularly, monotonously, said 'Open the door' but failed to add 'Richard' in the style of the popular song of the day.

Marriage to Susi was comforting. Knight had a public reputation for being a womanizer, a tag that maintained both his pride and his heterosexual status. But, exhausted by the war and threatened by Sillitoe's new arrangements, Knight found his heart trouble, which had begun when he was married to Gwladys, became more serious, developing into angina.

At forty-four he seemed old before his time and he welcomed a companion, someone to look after him and, to some extent, assuage his loneliness. Susi filled all his requirements beautifully, for she shared his love of nature and his interest in cricket and had a great admiration for his war work. Later she was to assert that Max could be very cruel, and there is no doubt that, as the marriage progressed, Knight began to distance parts of his personality from her, just as he had done with Gwladys, Lois and Joan. This time, however, he did not go away.

Knight still loved to play jazz on his clarinet and would invite friends in for jam sessions, accompanying jazz records and improvising drums from fire fenders, chairs, or anything else he could lay his hands on. But these were his good days; on bad ones he was becoming short-tempered and uneasy.

Eric St. Johnston used to visit M.I.5 in Curzon Street frequently on business and sometimes saw Knight.

'I knew him to be a very popular member of the staff but I think he was really, in the later years, regarded as a bit of a joke.' St. Johnston also remembers that now Knight was beginning to give lectures to Police Special Branch officers in different parts of the country on the Tyler Kent case.

At the end of the war, the personnel of B5(b) had been dispersed. Himsworth went abroad, the Wheatleys went back to their family, and Land and Poston departed. There had been two casualties: Brocklehurst had been drowned in Burma and Gillson was killed in an air crash after transferring to the S.O.E. Joan Miller, of course, was now married and working elsewhere. Of the original team, only Bingham and Younger remained. Knight now had one remaining case: he wanted to pursue his investigations into the growth of Soviet infiltration, despite the fact that he could find nobody to listen to him.

Then, in 1946, he received another personal blow. His sister Enid, who had been suffering for many years from a glandular problem, died of a brain tumour. She was fifty. Still devoted to her brother, Enid had never married but continued to run her dressmaking business from the flat in London where she lived in considerable poverty. Knight often went to see her in times of stress and she was one of the few who realized the extent of the façade that he kept up. Her secret was never to question but always to understand. He did not speak to his sister about his problems, but she shared much of his intuition. He was devastated by her death and came to rely more and more on the dependent, devoted Susi for moral support.

Special Branch officer Tom Roberts became a close friend and it is through his eyes that a vivid picture of the warmer side of Knight's personality can be seen.

'He loved children although he never had any of his own,' Roberts told me, 'and he would often come to our house to play with my children. At birthday parties he would appear as a magician, executing some very professional conjuring tricks that none of the Roberts family – or their guests – could possibly see through.'

Tom Roberts had first met Knight in 1942 at the Chief Constable of Surrey's office in Guildford, where Roberts was head of C.I.D. and Special Branch. He had many meals at the safe house in Camberley.

'Most of the Foreign Embassies had been moved out to avoid the bombing and Max wanted to keep tabs on what their staff were up to.'

Later he met Susi, summing her up as 'someone who was

deeply kind and understanding. Max always did things because it suited him to do them – but Susi was more sincere in her actions. Even so, if Max liked someone he would do everything for them, as many local police and C.I.D. officers knew to his credit in Camberley.'

Roberts used to go for long walks with Knight over the downs and found him a lake to fish in, 'although I had to tell him at the end of the day that I really hated fishing.' Knight talked to him a good deal about the dangers of Fascism at this stage, and told him how Dave Springhall had been arrested. But he never said a lot about the Communist threat. Roberts also visited Dolphin Square regularly.

'I used to go there for briefings – and I remember the flat with a lot of other people in it. I suppose they must have been his team of case officers.'

Roberts would do small jobs for Knight, such as warning an agent that he had committed an offence or investigating the backgrounds of people who were potential informers. He also remembered working in an office near David Cornwall (John Le Carré) in the early fifties. Cornwell, who knew Knight, later moved on to M.I.6. Another bond between Knight and Roberts was a strong interest in the occult.

'Max was always searching for other meanings to life, other reasons for being, and he used to discuss them with me avidly. He always seemed to be searching. He rarely mentioned his childhood, although he did tell me that his uncle in Glamorgan had been horsewhipped when a magistrate by a man he had convicted. Max also used to talk about Olga Gray and he was very high in his praise for her, including the fact that he said she was a remarkable graphologist.'

One of Knight's main contentions to Roberts was that M.I.5 officers should not interrogate when it became obvious that there would be a criminal charge, and this task should be carried out by the C.I.D. after sentencing.

When Malcolm Frost returned to the B.B.C. he was aware of

Knight's potential value to radio as a naturalist. He realized that Knight's charm came across in his speaking voice and his amazingly wide, if amateur, knowledge of natural history might be fascinating to the listeners. His plan was well-timed and some might say double-edged, as Sillitoe and Liddell thought that it would be better to phase Knight out slowly before they had to 'do a Kell' on him and that it would be more civilized to turn him gradually into a broadcasting pundit.

Knight broadcast for the first time in 1946 and immediately showed great aptitude for it. His cultured, resonant voice soon adapted itself to the requisite B.B.C. conventions and the carefully scripted talks suited him, as he had never been able to improvise. Careful planning and thinking round the problem were the tools of Knight's trade in M.I.5 and he applied the same skills to his broadcasting.

Beginning with such well-established programmes as the *Naturalist, Country Questions* and *Nature Parliament* (the latter aimed at children), Knight swiftly became a success. As Uncle Max on *Nature Parliament* he developed his own persona, a familiar, rich voice that exhorted children to become nature detectives, looking under logs, in hedgerows and in fields to discover the natural history world. Soon his audience was numbered in millions.

As a child John Cooper wrote to Knight about some aspect of natural history and was courteously answered. This began a series of visits to Knight's house (Cooper also lived in Camberley) in which Knight passed on to the boy a considerable amount of knowledge.

'He was part of the Sunday ritual – roast lamb and mint sauce, Max Knight on the radio and then a wonderful exploration of a pond or a wood before tea. Knight was a real amateur, concerned to encourage youngsters' interest in the natural environment around them. He had a bug room – an amazing place – in his house in Camberley and I was always taking specimens to him. We would spend hours poring over them. I was very flattered that he took so much interest in me – and I could never get over the fact that there I was talking to him when I had only just heard his voice on the radio. He was very famous then – a household name – and no-one could even have guessed at his past. He was known as Major Knight and I just knew he had had a distinguished war. Max Knight was an essential part of my childhood and his wife became godmother to my son – who I called Max.'

Now, thanks to Knight's inspiration, John Cooper is a distinguished international vet.

Knight was particularly fond of children, seemingly able to speak more directly to them than to adults and often communicating with then in the same way as he did with animals, creating the same instinctive bond of trust and understanding.

Life in Curzon Street was gradually becoming less and less rewarding. Knight continued to evangelize about the dangers of Communist infiltration, but it was just felt that he had a bee in his bonnet. It was not until the early 1950s that Knight was to see his predictions come true and by that stage it was too late for his career to be saved. As far as Sillitoe was concerned, Knight was a man of the past, a man of the old guard. Despite the fact that his warnings had been proved right, Sillitoe remained determined to try to avoid the kind of secrecy Knight had cultivated and that had become a mystique of the Burgess, Maclean and Philby defections. Sillitoe wrote: 'I myself would rather see two or three traitors slip through the net . . . than be a party to the taking of measures which could result in such a regime' (i.e. an executive which acted above the law). Knight fulminated at such measures, particularly when Sillitoe firmly stated: 'M.I.5 has no executive powers. And the head of the Security Service – fortunately in my opinion – is not empowered to take the law into its own hands and put people under arrest because he suspects them of being spies, or for any other reason.' This was a salient thought for Knight, as no doubt the disastrous Greene affair was very much in Sillitoe's mind when he made this point.

But the disappearance of Burgess, Maclean and Philby rocked

the world's confidence in M.I.5 and the British government. Sillitoe's system was now regarded as far too open. As a result, on the appointment of his successor, Dick White, in 1953, more secrecy became the order of the day.

But the advent of White was not to bring Knight back into the limelight. Derek Tangye, writing of Knight's 'The Comintern is not Dead' warning and its subsequent repetitions, said, 'The truth is that when I joined M.I.5 [at the beginning of the war], it was being geared to combat the Germans; and the Germans as an intelligence force had the rating of a Fourth Division football team. M.I.5 except in one small ignored corner of the organization [Knight's department] was bewildered when faced by the naughty deceit of the Russians.'[3]

When Dick White took over as Director-General in 1953, Liddell, in whose office Burgess had far too regularly been seen, retired to be Security Adviser to the Atomic Energy Authority and Roger Hollis, who had recently created the Security Intelligence Organization in Australia, became his Deputy. White, who was a graduate of Christ Church, Oxford, and also the universities of Michigan and California, had joined M.I.5 in 1936, becoming Assistant Director and then Director of B division in place of Liddell. He immediately set about trying to repair M.I.5's heavily dented image at home and abroad by a massive reorganization. This resulted in a new approach to vetting incoming staff as well as readjusting and realigning departments. D branch (formerly involved with agents and field investigations) took over counter-espionage, formerly the responsibility of B division, thus diminishing Knight's role even further. F division was already looking after infiltration into Fascist organizations and the C.P.G.B. and had tried to emulate Knight's brilliant operation with Olga Gray by using Betty Gordon, who spent ten years befriending Pollitt and regularly sending information back.

In 1953, Knight's Special Branch friend, Tom Roberts, was seconded to A division and later became a Police Liaison Officer.

[3] *The Way to Minack* (Michael Joseph, 1968).

'When I joined Max was a senior officer in F division and our offices were on the same floor, so I saw a lot of him. He hadn't felt Sillitoe was the right man for the job simply because he didn't have the necessary experience. But he liked and admired him – particularly for the rough, tough way Sillitoe had subdued the Glasgow gangs when he was Chief Constable there.'

Roberts also told me that Knight had a very high regard for Dick White, who was a man he had known for many years in M.I.5. He realized that White, unlike Sillitoe, had many years of experience of the job and that the old secrecy would return. Roberts said that White was astute and thought deeply before making a decision. He had been friendly with Max for many years.

Joan Miller's image of the ruthless case officer is somewhat allayed by Tom Roberts's remembrance of the Jimmy Dixon affair which occurred in 1953, the year Roberts joined M.I.5. Dixon was an agent who 'was beginning to look behind him' and Knight realized that he had to get rid of him. Instead of sacking and forgetting about him, Knight pensioned Dixon off, with an instruction to Roberts that he wanted someone to look after him.

'Max got him out on medical grounds,' remembered Roberts, 'and he would regularly come to tea with me and my wife. We tried to do as Max had said.'

Knight cast his net wide, believing in using every contact possible for maximum use, even when it came to trapping hedgehogs for his television programmes. One day Knight rang Tom Roberts and asked him urgently to find a· hedgehog. Although this was hardly a normal part of the job of a Special Branch officer, Roberts complied, putting out numerous bowls of milk in his back garden. Eventually, he dutifully captured the required hedgehog, rang Knight in triumph – and was told he had already got one. Roberts philosophically returned the hedgehog from whence it came. But this experience did not put him off.

'I have a great awareness of natural history now – entirely thanks to Max,' he admits. 'He would take me out to show me what owls lived on and we used to hunt for hours for their droppings. When found, Max would examine the pellets carefully, showing me the digested remains of mice and birds that the owl had recently eaten.'

Now Knight regularly turned to his broadcasting work for stimulation, appearing occasionally on television in such programmes as Peter Scott's *Look* and the famous *Animal, Vegetable or Mineral*. He wrote books on natural history and contributed regularly to magazines like *The Field* and *Country Life*. Then, in 1956, just at the end of White's tenure, Knight retired early from M.I.5 on grounds of poor health. It was true that his angina was worse, but in fact he was finding his work in the natural history world more interesting than M.I.5. He was awarded an O.B.E. and, at 55, abandoned his world of mystery and intrigue forever.

As a result Knight seemed to have remarkably little money – a situation which worried him greatly, but whether this was due to the fact that he had left M.I.5 before he had a full pension or possibly even to blackmail is not clear. Joan Miller suspects that Knight was being blackmailed, that someone was threatening exposure of his homosexuality, but there is no real evidence to prove that this was so. He had rented his house in Camberley, had miscalculated his income from freelance broadcasting and was extravagant, often lunching and dining out.

As Knight had never learnt to drive, it fell to Susi to take him from place to place, which helped to project a new image of Knight as a grand old man. Many years later, Susi told Winwood Reade, one of Knight's B.B.C. producers, that Joan had been Max's only mistake and that she (Joan) had been very bitter about the way she had been given up by Max. (This hardly matches Joan's version.) She went on to say that Knight had been cruel to her (by this she may have been alluding to his by now customary neglect), and that he was a spendthrift like his father; but she loved him very much.

Winwood Reade herself told me that towards the end of Susi's life she confided that it was awful not being able to let people know what Max had done for his country and what a wonderful person he was. But Susi had also signed the Official Secrets Act and the long period that her husband had spent as an M.I.5 case officer had to remain a closed book. This was deeply frustrating to Knight, who would have liked to write his autobiography, with specific reference to the fact that if his Comintern report had been believed then it is doubtful whether Burgess, Maclean, Philby and Blunt would have had such a long run or given away so many secrets.

Through the late forties, fifties and early sixties, Knight's career as a broadcaster and writer flourished and his connections with M.I.5 were totally severed. Although he kept the courtesy title of Major Knight, he gradually left behind his old persona of 'M', with cloak and dagger, hat and mackintosh. He kept his pipe, but became more genial and tweedy – an out-of-doors man that no-one would associate with the Buchan image he had once enjoyed. He also grew to believe in his new character, retaining only a few friends from the past such as Driberg, the Wheatleys and the Postons. He began to make friends in the natural history world who knew nothing about his previous career.

There was another aspect to Knight's full-time involvement with wild life, in strong contrast to the restraints of the past. Viscount Grey of Falloden wrote in his book *The Charm of Birds*: 'It is just because this wild life is amoral, not troubled by questions of right and wrong, that we find it so refreshing and restful.' Winwood Reade, herself a naturalist and now retired from the B.B.C.'s Natural History Unit, feels that 'the hedgerow, the field, the wood, and the animal kingdom are the only stable factors in an insecure, shifting world,' and certainly Knight's world in M.I.5 had been both insecure and shifting, masked as it was by all the bravado of intrigue. Such words as good, bad, right and wrong had lost their meaning to him after so many years of duplicity, but the animal kingdom did not recognize them either and this gave him a new feeling of freedom.

He generously helped others in the field, professionals or

amateurs. As an amateur himself, trying to make a freelance income to back up his pitifully small M.I.5 pension,[4] he still found time to preside over the politics of Camberley Natural History Society, as one of its members, Mrs. Hynd, remembers vividly:

'Above all he was charming – he couldn't help it. . . . We could always expect battle stations between the snake expert, Colonel Wilkins, and the butterfly man, Mr. Richards, but with the excellent control of Maxwell Knight, it became amusing swordplay between two enthusiasts.'

Knight had a laboratory at home with insect-breeding cages and some snakes, and he and Susi kept various odd pets. One of these was a mongoose which used to play in the living-room, emptying the waste-paper basket and hiding in it.

'I recall Susi telling me that she didn't like their bush-baby who was consistently incontinent when handled.'

Mrs. Hynd also remembers the Knights hand-rearing a young cuckoo, finally setting it free in the garden, from which it flew away after a few days.

Another new friend was the late James Fisher, a distinguished naturalist and writer, who felt that Knight was 'a sane and more effective version of the kind King Pellimore.' Pellimore was the fictional archetype of Knight's nature detective. In T. H. White's Arthurian books he is a comic figure, eternally on the trail of the Questing Beast. Knight used all his patience in detective work in the world of natural history. He could tell from a tattered pinecone whether it had been stripped by a squirrel, field mouse, woodpecker or crossbill and, when he found an empty nutshell, he would know whether a squirrel, mouse, doormouse, hawfinch or nuthatch had done the emptying. From the scraped bark or broken branch of a tree he could discover which species of deer had been involved – red, fallow or roe. He could trail and later identify virtually any kind of animal by their tracks, droppings, burrows, trails or scent. Knight's investigations included brilliant observation and

[4] Knight had retired early, thus forfeiting part of his pension.

deduction and, despite his amateur status, many professional naturalists began to regard him with respect.

Fisher's wife, Margery, remembers Knight in a different light.

'Max visited us here in the late forties or early fifties, as far as I recall. The visits were really to my husband, either possibly discussing one or other of the books for the young on birds which Max wrote, or just to have a weekend of bird-watching. Whatever the reason, we didn't see a lot of Max and I remember him as a rather silent but extremely amiable man. Perhaps with a houseful of children there weren't many chances for conversation anyway. The only moment I can recall when I discovered that Max was a great deal more than a bird-watcher was when for some reason we got on to the subject of jazz. (I had been a pupil at Oundle during the war with someone who was an enthusiast and through him I built up a small collection of Bix, Fats Waller *et al.*) Max told me something of his brief American experiences in World War I. This, as you can imagine, was extremely romantic, but I don't think I managed to persuade Max to enlarge on his past in this direction. Certainly, none of us knew then that he had been (and perhaps still was) an extremely important spy-master, though years later I did realize that this was perhaps the reason why he was so quiet and reserved.'

In the sixties Knight's nephew, Harry Smith, the son of Susi's sister Diana, was very close to his childless uncle.

'He used to talk to me a little about his work and continuously reminded me of the communist threat which he had frequently but unavailingly tried to bring to M.I.5's attention. His observation of the communists had begun early in the thirties, and he told me that he had only regarded the Nazis as a short term problem but the communists as a much more powerful menace. My uncle told me that fighting communism was like breaking the tail of a lizard; it would simply grow another. He was one of the first to suspect Blunt and felt that his disregarded warnings were vindicated when Burgess and Maclean defected.'

Smith also remembers that Knight was 'hopeless about

money', and that he turned down fronting an early dog-food commercial. 'I think he thought that it was undignified for the spymaster M to sell dog food on television.'

Smith saw his uncle as an extremely perceptive man with an effortless ability to assess people. But he felt Knight had failed to peak in both his careers, though it was an amazing achievement that he had been able to swop the job of spymaster for that of a popular naturalist and climb so far up the scale in both.

'He was worried about the student unrest in the sixties, believing it to be the perfect breeding ground for Russian infiltration. He ran his agents long after he had officially retired from M.I.5. I used to deliver mysterious parcels to them and I gathered that they would not work for anyone else except my uncle. He also told me that the Government were going to commission him to write the official history of M.I.5, but nothing seemed to come of it.'

Smith's last memories of his cricket-loving uncle were of frequent outings to Lord's, where they would share the summer hours with 'say, the chief coroner of Rochester and, very likely, a chief constable.' Smith shared his uncle's love of animals and would watch him indulging in his other passion – jazz – which he sometimes linked to the natural history world. 'He would try the effects of music on animals and he once played the clarinet to a swan.'

Deprived of secrecy and clandestine operation, Knight found the world of nature bringing him a great deal of comfort, for although it provided only a small income, it did attract considerable prestige. He was a council member of the Zoological Society of London, a Fellow of the Linnean Society, a council member and a member of the education committee of the Royal Society for the Protection of Birds, a founder and committee member of the Mammal Society, an associate of the Council for Nature, and an early member of the World Wildlife Fund, as well as serving on its Youth Advisory Council. In the mid-sixties he was also President of the British Naturalists' Association.

Dr. Ernest Neal, the world's leading expert on badgers,

remembers Knight as a 'professional communicator and an amateur naturalist'. He was among the first to film badgers, near his home at Camberley, but Neal noticed that there was always an element of touting for business and he suspected that Knight's self-confidence was beginning to slip. Neal did a great deal of broadcasting with him, mainly on the *Naturalist* programme, and he knew Knight liked to stick rigidly to his script. When this was altered or, worse still, when there was a need for him to ad-lib, he was immediately uneasy. Neal also remembers Knight's uncalculating generosity.

'I really couldn't help him professionally – and he knew this. Nevertheless, he put me up – and lobbied hard – for the Zoological Society's Stamford Raffles prize. I eventually won it in 1965.'

Knight became chairman of the *Naturalist* radio programme in the fifties. His avuncular voice continued as an essential accompaniment to Sunday lunch in millions of English homes. Only a very few remembered another more sinister context – when those same warm polished tones had interrogated spies or ordered the 'removal' of a double agent.

Tony Dale, a retired public relations officer of the London Zoo, was grateful to Knight for recommending him for the zoo job. He remembered him as 'a poor man for small talk,' at his happiest chatting about zoo affairs in the office or talking to the keepers. He seemed to have been a controversial member of the Zoological Society, full of new ideas and anxious to promote the zoo, which went down badly with more academic members who saw him as a popularist. Dale also knew that Knight loved making mischief on the committee.

'Personally, I felt that he regarded his marriage as no more than a partnership and I thought his wife, Susi, a lonely, distraught, sad woman. I also knew that Max could not accept being a has-been. I often felt that he had a greater love for the zoo than he had for his wife.'

But there were happier moments for the Knights' marriage, and some of these were spent with Leo Harrison Matthews,

Scientific Director of the London Zoo from 1951 to 1966, writer, broadcaster and international expert on whales.

'We had regular expeditions to Appledore on the Romney Marshes in Kent, at the end of May to hear the laughing frogs.' These were a particular breed of frog which made a laughing sound at night.

They would trek out over the marshes, catching the frogs in the beams of their torches and then returning to whisky and bread and cheese, left out in the kitchen by the wife of the landlord whose pub they were staying in. These were idyllic moments and it was at times like this that Susi felt closest to the elusive personality of her husband. Harrison Matthews remembers that 'I found Max a very loyal and devoted friend and he was never afraid to speak his mind at the zoo council. He was deeply interested in Communist infiltration and I remember Max asking me about the politics of some physicist I was working with.'

David McClintock, a naturalist specializing in wild flowers, also knew Max well in the fifties and sixties. 'He was very keen on gangster films and although I liked him enormously, I always felt he was on the make. Even when we were fishing, Max would always manage to get the best place on the river bank.'

Knight never really made the transition from radio to television, largely because, as Winwood Reade knew, he could not ad-lib. Knight had to be in a studio with a carefully prepared script from which he did not want to deviate. Outside location work, even for radio, made him uneasy, and talking to a camera was not something he could manage well. She remembers that he liked flirting with women but was discomforted when they came too close.

Another of his producers, Desmond Hawkins, later regarded as the founder of the B.B.C. Natural History Unit, had a very high regard for his abilities:

'His personal charm, which was considerable, was easily conveyed in his voice; he responded well to production and soon established himself as a dependable performer. . . . In addition to his achievement as a broadcaster, Max had in particular qualities that I valued in a chairman. He was well organized and delivered material punctually. He had a genuine courtesy in his handling of contributors and radiated a sympathetic reassurance which helped the nervous novices who formed an important element in our groups of speakers. . . . I never saw him flustered or ill at ease. He had the traditional qualities of the conventional gentleman of the pre-war world. . . . Outside our immediate preoccupations I had little insight into his life and character. I knew the bare fact of his involvement in Intelligence work, but I saw no reason to be inquisitive about it and he showed no inclination to talk about it. We must have formed at once a tacit understanding to ignore the subject; perhaps that contributed to the fact that, in retrospect, our relationship seems to have been so narrowly confined to the matter in hand.'

Knight's public life as a popular naturalist did not always work to a smooth plan. John Bingham remembers that, while demonstrating animals, a small bush-baby evaded Knight's restraining arms and escaped into the depths of the Army and Navy Stores. It was discovered only after an arduous hunt. He also remembers taking his daughter, Charlotte, to view some tarantula spiders Knight was keeping as pets. She was full of trepidation beforehand but was eventually disappointed because they were too small!

In the mid-sixties, Knight's angina was increasing and he was continually short of breath. He had become an old man. Always hampered by lack of money, he was forced to leave his house in Camberley and rent a smaller one. Then, in 1966, he and Susi moved to a wing of Guy Poston's house Josselyns, in Midgham, Berkshire, where Susi acted as housewife to the ailing Poston. There, Tom Roberts visited him and remembers that Max had slowed up badly and was showing his age. At this time, Pamela Wilson, headmistress of Downe House School, where Susi went to work after Knight's death, ame to know them both.

'Max by this stage,' she reflects, 'was not very well and the lectures he gave at my school were not up to his normal professional standards. Susi still drove him everywhere. She often appeared drab in Knight's company – but she blossomed out after he was dead. Susi was a person of the thirties who had that unique thirties gayness, a deceptive fragility and a strong will beneath.'

Pamela Wilson remembers Knight's interest in Aleister Crowley, as well as his bullying of Susi.

'He was very conscious of the impression he gave to other people and I thought he was very insecure.'

In 1968 Knight caught pneumonia. At first it seemed that there was little danger and he was cheerful in hospital. Susi had flu at the time and she was unable to visit him. Then, on Wednesday 27 January 1968, his already damaged heart could no longer take the strain of his difficult breathing and he died. He was sixty-eight.

Knight's memorial service was held at Saint James's Church, Piccadilly, on 20 February 1968 at 12 noon. Among the large congregation were a number of anonymous men whom no-one knew and who left immediately after the service. M.I.5 had come to pay its last respects. James Fisher gave the address, gently skating over Knight's career in M.I.5. All he said was:

'World War Two found him back in the forces, this time on the general staff at the War Office, where his deep insight into the character of people was specially used. Max's war job was a very difficult one, and could only have been done by one who was humane, honourable, decently strict and very intelligent.'

This bland statement was all that could be said of Knight's extraordinary career, and the grey men from M.I.5 nodded sagely – it was all that should be said. Fisher went on to describe Knight's public persona as a broadcaster and writer.

'Today is a sad day, but a proud day too, as we who loved Max ponder his enrichment of the world, and rejoice in the greatness of it. One of Max's books had the happy title *Bird*

Gardening. Max was one of the world's gardeners, and like most gardeners, one of the *kindest* men, who left his place – our place – better than he found it.'

The obituaries were equally bland. *The Times* on 1 February 1968 said: 'He was a skilled and agreeable broadcaster . . . a prolific and versatile author. . . . The visitor to his home at Camberley might find him nursing a bush-baby, feeding a giant toad, raising young cuckoos, or "engaging in masculine repartee with a vastly experienced grey parrot".'

On 2 February 1968, David McClintock added his own view in *The Times*: 'The death of Maxwell Knight, the Gay Cavalier of Natural History, cannot pass unmentioned. His charm, deep commonsense and great practical experience, particularly of animals of all kinds, meant he was widely known; and not only known, but an unfailing inspiration.'

Just before he died, Max had again used his detective skills in writing a children's book entitled *Be a Nature Detective*. This was published posthumously by Warne in May 1969, and commended in the *Times Educational Supplement*:

> The types of clues that are described are those involving tracking and identification of tracks, disturbed soil and vegetation, tell-tale traces of fur and feather, and remains of food and animal droppings. Sounds and smells are not neglected, and apart from bird song, the typical sounds made by a variety of animals are discussed together with hints on identification.
>
> The methods of walking silently, the ways to preserve tracks, how to dissect owl pellets, how and what to learn from an animal corpse are just a few of the suggestions and tips included in this book, and the final chapters discuss and pose some real-life problems for the readers to investigate.

Another accolade appeared in the form of an appeal in the *Countryside* magazine of autumn 1968 from a collection of Britain's most distinguished naturalists.

Dear Sir,

We, the undersigned, feel sure that many of your readers would wish to be made aware of the Maxwell Knight Memorial Fund.

Charles Henry Maxwell Knight, O.B.E., died in January in his sixty-eighth year. All his life he had an ardour for natural history, and for the last half of it wrote and spoke of animals with a dispassionate wisdom that brilliantly reflected his passionate enthusiasm.

In countless radio talks, television programmes and articles, and in a couple of dozen books Max Knight, born teacher and thoughtful researcher, communicated the message that man is one with nature, that man is a master of nature only by virtue of his study and understanding of it, and thus in the last analysis, servant to it. He was in the front rank of those who have led the Conservation movement in the middle third of the present century, and built the unity and strength of the organisations devoted to wild life.

Max's books, which will be read for years to come, are models of common sense, wisdom, integrity and enthusiasm, enlivened by gentle humour. They are a living memorial to him. We, old colleagues and old friends of his in Natural History and Conservation societies whose councils he so enriched, have arranged another commemoration.

We believe that the vast public whom Max inspired would wish to subscribe to the Conservation project bearing his name; and that because Max inspired so many people when they were still growing, this project should be educational. Susi Knight, Max's widow, agrees with us that this is what Max would have liked had his natural humility ever permitted this "perfect gentle Knight" to entertain the idea.

We ask, then, that those who would like to give, should subscribe to:

The Maxwell Knight Memorial Fund
WILDLIFE (The British National Appeal
of the World Wildlife Fund),
7–8 Plumptre Court
London. EC4.

Yours faithfully

[signed]	Desmond Hawkins
Priscilla Tweedsmuir	Humphrey Hewer
David Attenborough	Hurcomb
John Burton	Afred Leutscher
Maurice Burton	David McClintock
Aubrey Buxton	L. Harrison Matthews
Bruce Campbell	Johnny Morris
John Clegg	Peter Scott
Peter Conder	Landsborough Thomson
Cranbrook	Solly Zuckerman
James Fisher	
Richard Fitter	

Some years later, the Maxwell Knight Young Naturalists'
Library was established as a memorial to him and was housed in
the education centre of the Natural History Museum. Knight
would have been delighted with such a memorial – but an earlier
halt to the activities of Burgess, Maclean, Philby and Blunt
would perhaps have been more personally fulfilling.

Fourteen years later, Susi Knight lay dying of cancer in the Sue
Ryder Home in Oxfordshire. She had asked for a bed by a large
window so that she could use her field-glasses. Her remaining
pleasure was the one they had shared together: looking at
wildlife. From her bed she could see a bird-table and an expanse
of lawn where a green woodpecker and a muntjac deer gave her
particular delight. Not long before she died one of her visitors
brought her a water spider in a plastic bag, just to look at, and
she was enchanted. Perhaps Knight had not been able to give her

the love she needed, but what he had done was to allow her to share his abiding passion, the natural world.

There are two final epitaphs to the life of Maxwell Knight. The first is from John Bingham, his wartime colleague in B5(b) who knew him so well during the war years.

'Knight mothered his little brood of case officers in Dolphin Square, caring for us and his agents in a protective leadership that was fun as well as being exciting and dangerous. He was M.I.5's most brilliant case officer and we sorely miss those special days in Dolphin Square – when we were all Knight's Black Agents.'

The second is from Knight himself in another posthumously published book.[5] 'A becoming humility,' he wrote, 'is a great virtue where our relationship with animals is concerned, and it is the animal that pays you a compliment if it decides you are fit to know.'

A great many animals found Maxwell Knight fit to know, but the human animal was far more difficult – both less trusting and less trustworthy. On the whole, Knight preferred the former.

[5] *Pets and their Problems* (Heinemann Medical Books, 1968).

POSTSCRIPT

As soon as my research on Knight's life was known to the Office (as M.I.5 is known to its employees) a 'welfare officer' visited Susi at the Sue Ryder Home, forbidding her to discuss Knight with me and ordering the staff to refuse me entry. Later, an establishment officer from the War Office officially wrote to Susi, reminding her that she had signed the Official Secrets Act and must on no account talk to her husband's biographer. This, plus press allegations of Knight's homosexuality by Joan Miller in the *Sunday Times* and by Nigel West in his history of M.I.5,[1] troubled her greatly, yet no-one in M.I.5 offered her any comfort. The British Government has always been bedevilled by secrecy and M.I.5 had laid its bureaucratic shroud on Susi. She died in considerable disquiet on 29 January 1983.

[1] *M.I.5: British Security Service Operations 1909–1946* (Bodley Head, 1981).

BIBLIOGRAPHY

Apart from the published sources listed below, some of the material quoted in this book has been taken from documents recently released by M.I.5. In addition, after much research into their present whereabouts, I was able to interview many of Knight's friends and associates and members of his family, who generously gave me permission to include quotations from these interviews. Unpublished material on the Ben Greene case is quoted by kind permission of Paul and Edward Greene.

Acton, Harold. *More Memoirs of an Aesthete* (Methuen, 1970)
Bingham, John. *The Double Agent* (Dutton, 1967)
Boyle, Andrew. *The Climate of Treason* (Hutchinson, 1979)
Buchan, John. *The Thirty-Nine Steps* (Hodder & Stoughton, 1915)
 Greenmantle (Hodder & Stoughton, 1916)
 Memory Hold the Door (Hodder & Stoughton, 1940)
Bullock, John. *M.I.5: the Origin and History of the British Counter Espionage* (Arthur Barker, 1963)
Costello, John. *The Pacific War* (Warne, 1981)
Churchill, Winston S. *The Second World War Vol. I. The Gathering Storm* (Cassell, 1948)
 Vol. II. Their Finest Hour (Cassell, 1949)
Clark, Jon, and others. *Culture and Crisis in Britain in the 30's* (Lawrence & Wishart, 1979)
Deacon, Richard. *A History of the British Secret Service* (Muller, 1969)
Driberg, Tom. *Ruling Passions* (Jonathan Cape, 1977)
Fitzgibbon, Constantine. *Secret Intelligence in the 20th Century* (Hart-Davis MacGibbon, 1976)

BIBLIOGRAPHY

Gillman, Peter and Leni. *Collar The Lot* (Quartet, 1980)

Greene, Graham. *A Sort of Life* (Bodley Head, 1971)

Griffiths, Richard. *Fellow Travellers of the Right: British Enthusiasts for Nazi Germany 1933–39* (Constable, 1980)

Harwell, Jock. *Spies and Spymasters* (Thames & Hudson, 1977)

Knight, Maxwell, *Be A Nature Detective* (Warne, 1969)

    Crime Cargo (Philip Allan, 1934)

    Gunman's Holiday (Philip Allan, 1935)

    Pets and their Problems (Heinemann, 1968)

    The Young Naturalist's Field Guide (G. Bell, 1952)

Masterman, J.C. *The Double Cross System in the War of 1939–1945* (Yale University Press, 1972).

Modern Public Records: the Report of a Committee Appointed by the Lord Chancellor (H.M.S.O., 1981)

Modern Public Records: a Government Response to the Report of the Wilson Committee (H.M.S.O., 1982)

Mosley, Nicholas. *Rules of the Game: Sir Oswald and Lady Cynthia Mosley 1896–1953* (Secker & Warburg, 1983)

    Beyond the Pale (Secker & Warburg, 1983)

Mosley, Sir Oswald. *My Life* (Nelson, 1968)

Page, Bruce, and others. *Philby: the Spy who Betrayed a Generation* (André Deutsch, 1968)

Pimlott, Ben. *Labour and the Left in the 1930's* (Cambridge University Press, 1977)

Pincher, Chapman, *Their Trade is Treachery* (Sidgwick & Jackson, 1981)

St. Johnston, Eric. *One Policeman's Story* (Barry Rose, 1978)

Seale, Patrick, and McConville, Maureen. *Philby: The Long Road To Moscow* (Hamish Hamilton, 1973)

Skidelsky, Robert. *Oswald Mosley* (Macmillan, 1975)

Sutherland, Douglas. *The Fourth Man* (Secker & Warburg and Arrow Books, 1980)

Symonds, John. *The Great Beast: the Life and Magick of Aleister Crowley* (Macdonald, 1971)

Symons, Julian. *The Thirties: a Dream Resolved* (Cresset Press, 1960)

Tangye, Derek. *The Way to Minack* (Michael Joseph, 1968)

Thompson, R.W. *Churchill and Morton: Correspondence between Major Sir Desmond Morton and R.W. Thompson* (Hodder & Stoughton, 1976)

BIBLIOGRAPHY

Toland, John. *Infamy: Pearl Harbour and its Aftermath* (Methuen, 1982)

West, Nigel. *M.I.5: British Security Service Operations 1909–1946* (Bodley Head, 1981)

    A Matter of Trust: M.I.5 1943–72 (Weidenfeld, 1982)

West, Rebecca. *The Meaning of Treason* (Macmillan, 1949)

Wheatley, Dennis. *The Young Man Said: Memoirs 1897–1914* (Hutchinson, 1977)

    Drink and Ink: Memoirs 1919–1977 (Hutchinson, 1979)

    Stranger Than Fiction (Hutchinson, 1959)

INDEX